SO-AIN-758

Iris Schreier's
REVERSIBLE
KNITS

Iris Schreier's
REVERSIBLE KNITS

Creative Techniques for Knitting Both Sides Right

Iris Schreier

An Imprint of Sterling Publishing
387 Park Avenue South
New York, NY 10016

First Paperback Edition 2013
Text © 2009, Iris Schreier
Photography © 2009, Lark Books, an Imprint of Sterling Publishing Co., Inc.;
unless otherwise specified
Illustrations © 2009, Lark Books, an Imprint of Sterling Publishing Co., Inc.;
unless otherwise specified

ISBN 978-1-60059-117-4 (hardcover) 978-1-4547-0842-1 (paperback)

The Library of Congress has cataloged the hardcover edition as follows:

Schreier, Iris.
  [Reversible knits]
  Iris Schreier's reversible knits : creative techniques for knitting both sides right.
      p. cm.
  Includes index.
  ISBN 978-1-60059-117-4 (hc-plc with jacket : alk. paper)
  1. Knitting. I. Title.
  TT820.S297 2009
  746.43'2—dc22

                          2008033522

Distributed in Canada by Sterling Publishing
c/o Canadian Manda Group, 165 Dufferin Street
Toronto, Ontario, Canada M6K 3H6
Distributed in the United Kingdom by GMC Distribution Services
Castle Place, 166 High Street, Lewes, East Sussex, England BN7 1XU
Distributed in Australia by Capricorn Link (Australia) Pty. Ltd.
P.O. Box 704, Windsor, NSW 2756, Australia

For information about custom editions, special sales, and premium
and corporate purchases, please contact Sterling Special Sales at
800-805-5489 or specialsales@sterlingpublishing.com.

Email academic@larkbooks.com for information about desk and examination
copies. The complete policy can be found at larkcrafts.com.

Every effort has been made to ensure that all the information in this book
is accurate. However, due to differing conditions, tools, and individual skills,
the publisher cannot be responsible for any injuries, losses, and other
damages that may result from the use of the information in this book.

Manufactured in China

2 4 6 8 10 9 7 5 3

larkcrafts.com

SENIOR EDITOR:
SUZANNE J.E. TOURTILLOTT

EDITORS:
LARRY SHEA AND NATHALIE MORNU

ART DIRECTOR:
DANA M. IRWIN

ART PRODUCTION:
KAY HOLMES STAFFORD

TECHNICAL EDITOR:
JUDITH DURANT

ILLUSTRATOR:
ORRIN LUNDGREN

PHOTOGRAPHERS:
STEWART O'SHIELDS AND STEWART YOUNG

COVER DESIGNER:
SHANNON YOKELEY

To my husband and boys,
who make it all worthwhile

contents

MASTER MORE METHODS

ONLINE!
Explore more of my exclusive bonus content online at
www.larkcrafts.com/bonus

Written instructions, keyed charts, and video show you how!

My shelves are full of knitting books with beautiful stitch patterns, but almost none of them give any indication of how the reverse side of a knitted piece should look. It's an accepted fact that if you're going to knit a sweater, or mittens, or a cap, it will have a "right" side and a "wrong" side. I wanted patterns that are pretty on both sides, and in my search for ways to create pieces with two beautiful faces to show the world, I eventually realized that the answers had to come from my own two hands. And now you hold my discoveries in yours.

So how can a knitted piece be made reversible? For me, the design has to be intentional, so that both sides are beautiful and balanced. Reversibility isn't only about turning a piece inside out, like a cheap nylon jacket. Reversible knitting is much more than that! If both knitted sides are similar—or even completely different from each other—the piece is reversible in a way that most knitwear is not. Either side can be "public." And here's the good news: the adjustments you'll have to make to your usual knitting techniques are usually quite simple. This book shows you how to do it. To be successful with the projects you'll find here, all you need to know is how to knit, purl, increase, decrease, and (of course) cast on and bind off.

In the Basics section, you'll start off with a quick survey of the best types of yarns, needles, and notions needed for this kind of knitting. I used my own brand of yarn (and lots of different fiber types) for all the projects, but you can easily substitute other brands and fibers by referring to the Yarn Substitution Chart on page 142. This introductory section also explains a number of techniques—knitting in the round, two-color knitting, modular knitting, and others—with an eye toward how to employ them in the reversible knitting projects that follow.

Six chapters highlight key techniques: One-Yarn and then Multi-Yarn Knit/Purl, Lace, Cable, Double Knitting, and Modular. Each chapter begins by introducing related techniques, all accompanied by front-and-back swatch photos to let you see what the knitted fabric should look like on both sides. After that, you get to the fun part of the chapter: several gorgeous projects that you'll love to make. Are you fairly new to knitting (or simply new to reversible knitting)? No problem—just keep in mind that the first projects in each chapter are the easier ones, and the later ones more challenging.

You'll discover in the first chapter how, with a single yarn, you can create pieces with two identical sides as well as ones with sides that are quite different, though equally attractive. You'll be introduced to the all-important rib pattern, which creates an accordion-like knitted fabric in which all elements you wish to keep private can be buried in front of hidden purl bumps. The Multi-Yarn chapter reveals the possibilities inherent with two-strand reversible knitting, with tips for changing colors that achieve dramatic and lovely effects on both sides.

After that, two chapters present ideas for incorporating reversible Lace and Cable techniques into your work. You'll learn, for example, how to use circular knitting methods to create both different-sided and like-sided pieces. The Double Knitting chapter offers two ways to achieve a double-sided fabric with two yarns. You'll find yourself knitting on both sides of the piece at the same time and hiding "undesired" strands of color in between.

In contrast, the Modular projects in the sixth chapter are all knitted angularly and in Garter or Stockinette and Reverse Stockinette stitches. You'll learn to create geometric shapes in your knitting that are completely

seamless. Traditional modular designs always have seams on one side, but here you'll discover ways to achieve true reversibility.

Initially I intended for this book to be just a compilation of various techniques, each showcased with complementary projects. But somehow, while putting together samples of stitch patterns, I stumbled across possibilities I had never seen anywhere else. And that's how the final section of the book came to be: a collection of unique stitch combinations titled More Techniques to Explore. The swatches you'll see there combine techniques from the earlier chapters to create six new and innovative designs. There are cables that are different on both sides and in different colors. Double knitting combined with lace creates some truly different "thick and thin" designs.

From the experience you'll gain through this book, I hope to inspire you to use these techniques in your other knitting projects, not just in the pieces you find here. For further inspiration, check out my bonus techniques and information at www.larkbooks.com/crafts. Continue to explore reversible knitting, and enjoy the moment when somebody looks at a piece you've made and asks in admiration: "How on earth did you do that?"

The Basics

How to Use This Book

This book presents six key techniques in reversible knitting: single- and multi-strand methods, lace, cables, double knitting, and modular construction. Each chapter demonstrates how the key technique can be made reversible with a series of swatches, complete with instructions for hands-on exercises and tips for incorporating the technique into your own unique reversible designs. Following the exercises, you'll find a variety of patterns that showcase the various techniques. The later chapters include projects that combine multiple techniques from several categories.

The patterns range from beginner to intermediate and beyond. I determined the skill level by taking into account several factors, including the number and type of yarns used. Generally, a finer yarn demands greater experience than a heavier one, and juggling more than one yarn at a time requires some knitting expertise. The projects are ranked relative to one another, so don't be put off by intermediate or advanced ratings.

For example, if you have successfully mastered double knitting the intermediate-level Ribbon Candy Scarf on page 102, I encourage you to knit the advanced Southport Shawl on page 107, even though you may not consider yourself an advanced knitter.

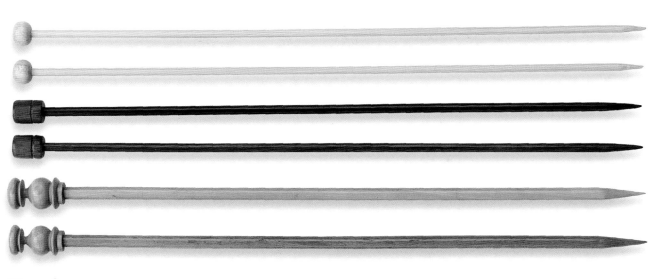

Tools

The hundreds of types of knitting needles and other tools that are on the market today cater to every possible taste. Very experienced knitters may enjoy the delightful banquet, but if you're new to the field, here are some guidelines for the tools you'll need to work the projects in this book.

Needles

Wood needles provide excellent control because of the fairly high surface tension between wood and yarn; there's a bit of drag there, even though the wood is smooth. Choose wood for more slippery yarns such as silks. By contrast, confident knitters might prefer nickel or aluminum needles—yarn slides easily on these surfaces, and with less drag, more speed is possible. Experiment by knitting with various types of needles and different fibers. You may find that you prefer to use wood needles with more slippery yarn such as silk, and metal needles with coarser yarn such as wool.

Projects that are knit in the round will require circular needles. Look for those with the smoothest connecting join between the needle tips and the cable. If the join is rough, your stitches may catch on it and you'll be constantly tugging at your work. Replace needles that don't provide smooth sailing for your stitches.

Choose the shortest practical needle length for your project—this applies to straight, circular, and double-pointed needles alike. Small projects, such as the Riff Belt on page 52, are ideally suited for $5\frac{1}{2}$-inch/14cm double-pointed needles. Because the rows are short, it's quicker to turn and knit the rows on shorter needles than on longer ones that can get in the way. In some projects that are knit in the round you'll be working with a small numbers of stitches, so you'll need fairly short, 16-inch/40cm, circular knitting needles. You could also use double-pointed needles (some knitters use two circular needles to achieve the same effect). The La Parisienne Collar and the Charcoal Möbius Collar projects on pages 66 and 104 require circular needles that are long enough to go around the circumference of the project twice—a minimum of 40-inch/100cm in length.

Double knitting or slip stitch knitting will sometimes produce uneven elongated stitches. Go down a needle size from the recommended size for these projects or experiment with a variety of needles. Use circular or double-pointed needles whenever projects use slip stitch knitting and require that the stitches slide from one end to the other to carry up a second yarn.

NEEDLE CONVERSION CHART

Metric (mm)	U.S.	Metric (mm)	U.S.
2	0	5.5	9
2.25	1	6	10
2.5	1	6.5	10½
2.75	2	7	10½
3	3	8	11
3.25	3	9	13
3.5	4	10	15
3.75	5	12	17
4	6	15	19
4.25	6	19	35
4.5	7	20	36
5	8	25	50

Stitch Holders

Stitch holders are required for some projects. When you need to knit on only some of the stitches, place the other stitches on a holder to keep them out your way. Use the lightest weight stitch holders you can find to prevent them from dragging and stretching the stitches out of shape. You can also use a piece of contrasting-color scrap yarn to hold the stitches in place. Thread a tapestry needle with the scrap yarn and draw it through the stitches to be held. Make sure the piece of scrap yarn is sufficiently long that the ends can be tied together in a large loop.

Stitch Markers

Some projects call for stitch markers. Those made like safety pins without the coil are ideal—they won't move around or snag your knitting.

Save money on holders and markers so you can afford the best needles. Finely crafted needles help you to knit smoothly and with pleasure—you do want to have fun doing this!

Yarns and Yarn Substitutions

Although following the instructions exactly for the designs included in this book will ensure good results, I urge more experienced knitters to consider them as starting points. Try other yarns and feel free to make modifications to the patterns. If the design doesn't look right with the substitute yarn you've chosen, experiment by making small swatches with different stitch combinations, or put together unexpected color combinations. I've shown close-up photos of the individual strands of yarn used in every project to guide you in creating your own versions.

Characteristics such as the weight, elasticity, drape, luster, hand, and texture (see Terms of Endearment, page 16) all play a role in determining what sort of pattern works best with which yarn. Use the instructions in the exercises at the beginning of each chapter to create swatches in a variety of yarns. This will help you choose the kind of yarn to use with each type of design. Here are some general tips:

■ Simple, smooth yarns provide better stitch definition than fuzzy ones, and they show off your hard work when you create a two-sided piece.

■ For designs that produce two layers of knitted fabric, such as the Tiger's Paw Scarf on page 80 or Nordic Tracks Hoodie on page 55, choose fine and extremely soft yarns. These could be mohair, cashmere, or lightweight silk. Avoid wools and coarse or stiff yarns, because the drape and hand of the piece will suffer.

The Yarn Substitution Chart on page 142 will help you to identify appropriate yarn substitutions for the Artyarns yarns used in the book.

Silk

Cashmere

Merino wool

Silk and mohair with glass beads

Silk and cashmere

Yarn Care

Care for luxury fibers by hand washing carefully with a mild soap specifically meant for fine washables. Don't wring them, but after soaking in a cool, mild soap bath and rinsing, roll knitted items in a towel and carefully lay them on a flat surface to dry completely without being moved. To block luxury yarns, use a hand steamer. If you do use an iron, make sure to place a protective cloth, such as a dish towel, between the hot iron and the knitted fabric. Follow the label instructions for wools, as these can generally be machine or hand washed, and dried flat.

General Knitting Techniques

This section includes a review of standard techniques that are used in this book. Most of the techniques described are commonly used in many knitting patterns today.

Knitting in the Round

Sounds fun, right? It is! This knitting method is done with either circular needles or double-pointed ones. I explain their mysteries here.

CIRCULAR NEEDLES

For knitting in the round, a pair of wooden or metal needles are joined by a flexible plastic cable. You cast on stitches as usual, but at the end of the row, instead of flipping the piece and switching it back to your dominant hand as you do in straight knitting, you join the beginning and ending stitches and start the first round by knitting into your first cast-on stitch. Double-check to ensure that the stitches aren't twisted before you join the work (see figure 1). Always use a marker to identify the beginning of a round and help you keep track in your pattern. The stitch marker is slipped (transferred from one needle to the other) to maintain its position.

DOUBLE-POINTED NEEDLES

Five straight needles with points on both ends can be used to knit in the round. The stitches are divided equally onto four of the needles, and you knit with the fifth needle. When stitches are knitted off a needle, that needle becomes the extra needle that is used to knit the next group of stitches in order. Use double-pointed needles when the circumference of the work is less than 16 inches/40.5 cm—this is the smallest length circular needle that is available and comfortable to use. For example, a hat pattern that is knitted in the round requires that you change to double-pointed needles once the number of stitches has been decreased for the top of the hat. You could use

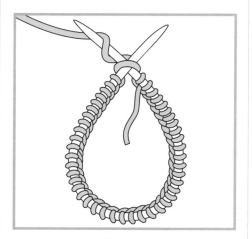

figure 1

double-pointed needles throughout the hat project, but they are more awkward to manage than a circular needle.

Because the knitting is being worked circularly in rounds, rather than back and forth in rows, the resulting fabric when all stitches are knitted is Stockinette—whereas in straight knitting, when all stitches are knitted the resulting fabric is Garter. Several projects in this book are knitted in the round to create a double-sided reversible fabric.

Two-Color Knitting

There are many ways to use two or more colors in your knitting. Here are some techniques for using two colors in reversible knits.

CHANGING COLORS IN STRAIGHT KNITTING

When knitting with two colors, it's important to be consistent about how you change from one color to the other.

14

Always carry yarn A up from behind yarn B (see figure 2). If you do this consistently, you'll have nice neat edges. When one yarn is used for four or more rows and a second yarn must be carried up the side, proceed as follows. After two rows of A, carry B up and twist it completely around A before resuming with A. Don't carry yarn up for more than two rows or an unsightly loop will form.

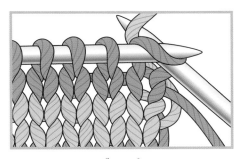

figure 2

SMOOTH COLOR CHANGES

When colors are changed in Stockinette or Garter stitch, whether you're knitting back and forth or in the round, bumps appear in the contrasting color on the wrong side of the fabric (as shown below).

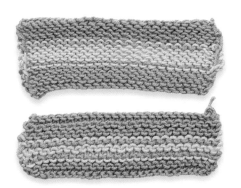

Because both sides of the fabric will show in reversible knits, you'll want to minimize this interruption. Some methods used to avoid this include changing color in rib patterns (see page 43), changing color using the Interrupted Garter Pattern (see page 113), or using lace faggoting patterns (see page 60).

Vertical bumps in contrasting colors also appear on one side when colors are changed in the middle of a row (as shown above). These bumps can be prevented by using decreases to join two colors that are switched in the center of the work (see page 42).

TERMS
OF ENDEARMENT

New to knitting? Learn these terms and sound like a pro. Words that describe fiber weight can seem idiosyncratic: *light weight* is obvious, but what about *worsted* or *sport*? Yarn category is determined by the *gauge* of the yarn, or how many stitches can be counted horizontally, and how many rows can be counted vertically in a 4-inch/10cm knitted square. The *thicker* the yarn, the fewer stitches and rows per inch, and the *thinner* the yarn, the more stitches and rows per inch. The Craft Yarn Council of America provides a handy guide to yarn weights (see below).

The amount of stretch in a yarn is called *elasticity*. How the knitted piece hangs is its *drape*. *Luster* will describes the external shine that the yarn has, while *hand* deals with the feel of the knitted cloth. *Texture* is used to refer to fuzziness or bumpiness.

Yarn Weight Symbol & Category Names	**0** LACE	**1** SUPER FINE	**2** FINE	**3** LIGHT	**4** MEDIUM	**5** BULKY	**6** SUPER BULKY
Types of Yarns in Category	Fingering, 10-count crochet thread	Sock, Fingering, Baby	Sport, Baby	DK, Light Worsted	Worsted, Afghan, Aran	Chunky, Craft, Rug	Bulky, Roving
Knit Gauge Range in Stockinette Stitch to 4 inches (10.2 cm)	33–40 sts	27–32 sts	23–26 sts	21–24 sts	16–20 sts	12–15 sts	6–11 sts
Recommended Metric Needle Size	1.5–2.25 mm	2.25–3.25 mm	3.25–3.75 mm	3.75–4.5 mm	4.5–5.5 mm	5.5–8 mm	8 mm and larger
Recommended U.S. Needle Size	000 to 1	1 to 3	3 to 5	5 to 7	7 to 9	9 to 11	11 and larger

Casting On and Binding Off

There are a lot of ways to cast on and bind off. Here are the methods you'll use for the projects in this book.

KNITTED-ON CAST-ON

This method can be used to begin a project, and it also allows you to add new stitches to existing stitches you've already been knitting. If you don't already have stitches on your needle, cast on one stitch by placing a slip knot on the needle and hold the needle in your left hand.

Insert the right needle into the first stitch on the left needle as if to knit it. Knit the stitch, but don't drop the stitch from the left needle. Place the newly knitted stitch back on the left needle (see figure 3).

figure 3

Continue adding new stitches in this manner until you have added as many stitches as the pattern calls for.

LONG-TAIL CAST-ON

Leaving a tail long enough to cast on the required number of stitches (1 inch per stitch is plenty), make a slip knot and place it on the needle. *Wrap one yarn around your thumb and the other around your index finger. Hold the long ends with your other three fingers (see figure 4).

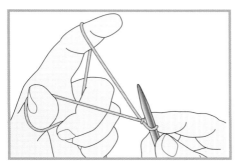

figure 4

Insert the needle into the loop around your thumb from front to back and over the yarn around your index finger (see figures 5 and 6).

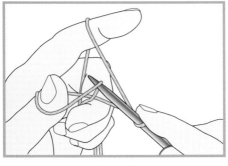

figure 5

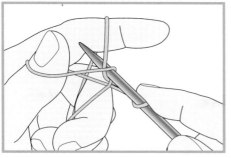

figure 6

Bring the needle down through the loop on your thumb (see figure 7).

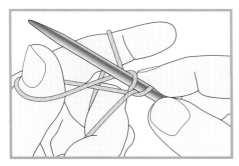

figure 7

Drop the loop off your thumb and tighten the stitch. Repeat from * for the required number of stitches.

PROVISIONAL CAST-ON

A provisional cast-on allows you to knit from both sides of each cast-on stitch (top and bottom). Once you've knitted a few rows, the stitches can be put back on needles and knitted in the other direction. A smooth contrasting color scrap yarn can easily be identified and undone to expose the live stitches.

Using a crochet hook and smooth scrap yarn, chain the number of stitches called for in the pattern plus an additional five or so. On one side of the chain, the stitches form Vs, and on the other side of the chain, the stitches form bumps. Insert the knitting needle into the bump of the stitch next to the one forming the loop on hook and knit it (see figure 8).

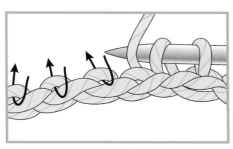

figure 8

Continue along the chain, knitting into each following bump, until you have the number of stitches required by the pattern. Now attach the main knitting yarn and start to knit following the instructions for the project. After several rows of knitting, or when instructed in the pattern, remove the scrap yarn and carefully transfer the live stitches at the bottom edge to a knitting needle. You'll now be able to work these stitches in the other direction.

CASTING ON TO A BELT RING

Using a provisional cast-on (see page 17), cast on a suitable number of stitches to cover the belt ring surface or the number of stitches specified in the pattern. Knit several rows. Transfer the provisional stitches onto a short double-pointed needle. Slip the belt ring onto the center of knitting as shown in figure 9. If there is a prong, insert it into the center of the knitted piece. Wrap the knitted piece around the ring and join the provisional stitches with the knitted stitches as follows: Using a third needle, *k2tog (top stitch from needles 1 and 2), leaving the resulting stitch on the third needle. Repeat from * until all stitches are on needle 3.

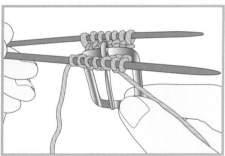

figure 9

MÖBIUS CAST-ON

A Möbius is a never-ending twisted loop that is created when a circular needle is used with the cable coiled. Use the long-tail cast-on method to attach stitches to the top and bottom of your piece at the same time. Every stitch that you cast on will actually result in a double stitch—the top of the stitch will be on the needle, and the bottom of the stitch will be on the coil.

Use an extra-long circular needle (a minimum of 36 inches/91cm). Wrap the cable into a coil and hold the right needle tip and cable in your right hand. Leaving a long tail for casting on, make a slip knot and place it on the needle so that the tail and the working yarn are in front of the cable. With your left hand, reach under the cable from behind and pick up the tail and the working yarn, holding them in position for the long-tail cast-on. With your thumb in front of the cable, your index finger behind the cable, and the cable resting between your thumb and index finger, cast on the first stitch (figure 10).

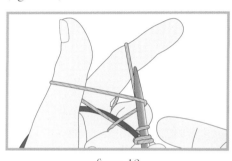

figure 10

To cast on the next stitch, bring your thumb and the loop of yarn through the coil to the back of the cable (see figure 11).

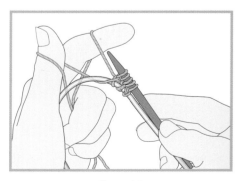

figure 11

Continue casting on by alternately placing your thumb under and in front of the cable, then under and behind the cable, until you have the number of stitches specified in the pattern. When you're ready to knit the first round, place a marker to identify the start of the round, as in ordinary circular knitting. On the first half of the stitches, every other stitch will appear as a twisted stitch—one stitch will lean away from the tip of the needle and the stitch following it will lean toward the tip of the needle. Knit (or purl) the stitches leaning away from the tip of the needle through the front of the stitch as usual, but knit (or purl) the stitches leaning toward the tip of the needle through the back of the stitch to untwist them. Figure 12 shows how to knit through the back part of the stitch when the stitch is leaning toward the tip of the needle. Note that the next stitch is leaning away from the tip of the needle, and therefore it will be knitted in the regular manner. The remaining half of the stitches will appear as ordinary stitches, so knit (or purl) those as usual through the front part of the stitch.

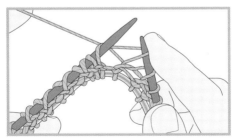

figure 12

THREE-NEEDLE BIND-OFF

Three-needle bind-off is used to join two pieces together while binding off, eliminating the need to sew seams.

figure 13

With the right sides of the knitted fabric that you're joining facing each other, hold the two needles together in your left hand. With a third needle in your right hand, knit two stitches together, working one stitch from the front needle and one stitch from the back needle. *Knit next two stitches together as before, taking one stitch from the front and one from the back. Pass the previous stitch worked over the latest stitch worked to bind off. Repeat from * until all stitches have been bound off (figure 13).

Double Knitting

Double knitting as it's used in this book creates a two-layered reversible fabric with knit stitches facing out on both sides of the work. You'll knit on both sides at the same time, using two different color yarns.

Two-Strand Method

In some projects colors A and B are used together to cast on. Whenever AB is specified in the instructions, knit or purl with both strands together. Whenever A or B are specified separately, knit or purl with the individual strands. The most important thing to remember is that when knitting, you should bring both strands to the back, and when purling bring both strands to the front (see figures 14 and 15).

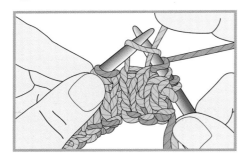

figure 14

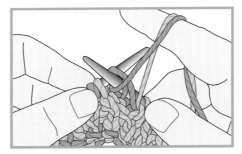

figure 15

When knitting the first row, you'll sometimes be required to create two stitches from each of the cast-on stitches. Do this by knitting into the front of the stitch with A, and knitting into the back of the same stitch with B (or the colors specified in the pattern).

If you've never used this technique before, practice with two identical yarns in two contrasting colors to create a swatch as follows:

Cast on 20 stitches with A.

Hold two strands together, one of each color (A and B).

Row 1: *K1A, p1B; repeat from * to end of row.

Row 2: Twist A around B to seal edge, *k1B, p1A; repeat from * to end of row.

Row 3: Twist B around A to seal edge, *k1A, p1B; repeat from * to end of row.

Repeat rows 2 and 3 and you'll see how you've created two separate layers of fabric at the same time.

Slip Stitch Method

Slipping stitches is simply transferring them from one needle to the other without knitting them. The major consideration is whether to slip the stitch by carrying the working yarn in front of or in back of the knitted piece. The instructions will indicate sl 1b (slip 1 stitch with yarn in back) or sl 1f (slip one stitch with yarn in front). Using this method, you can knit a hollow tube on straight needles with only one yarn. Cast on an even number of stitches and alternate between knit one stitch, and slip the next stitch with the yarn in front across the row. Repeat this on every row, take the knitting off the needles, and you'll see that you've created a tube.

When using two colors, the slip stitch method can be less awkward than the two-strand method, and it produces similar results. However, it is slower than the two-strand method because every row must be worked twice. Practice with two identical yarns in two contrasting colors to create a swatch as follows:

Cast on 20 stitches with A on double-pointed needles. Slide the stitches to the other end of the needle to work B.

Row 1: Attach B. With B, *s1 1b (transfer 1 stitch from left to right needle with yarn in back), p1; repeat from * to end of row. Turn to work A.

Row 2: Twist A over and around B to seal the edge, with A, *s1 1b, p1; repeat from * to end of row. Slide stitches to other end of needle to work B.

Row 3: With B, *k1, s1 1f (transfer 1 stitch from left to right needle with yarn in front); repeat from * to end of row. Turn to work A.

Row 4: Twist A over and around B to seal the edge, with A, *k1, s1 1f; repeat from * to end of row. Slide stitches to the other side of the needle to work B.

Row 5: With B, *s1 1b, p1; repeat from * to end of row. Turn to work A.

Repeat rows 2–5.

Follow the instructions in the pattern for knitting with yarn A, slipping every other stitch by transferring it from one needle to the other as if to knit with the yarn in back (see figure 16), then sliding the stitches to the other end of the needle to pick up yarn B. Continue to knit with yarn B, slipping every other stitch by transferring it from one needle to the other as if to purl with the yarn in front (see figure 17). Now both yarn A and B are on the same side. Twist A over B and begin row 2 with A.

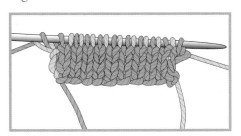

figure 16

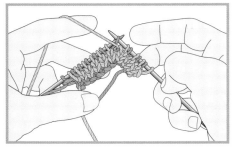

figure 17

Changing Colors in Double Knitting

To seal and produce neat edges, twist the yarns at the beginning of the row when changing colors in double knitting. If the last stitch in a row was knitted with yarn A and now the same stitch in the next row will be worked in yarn B, twist B *under* A to start knitting with B. By contrast, if yarn A is to be used again on the next row, twist B *over* A to start knitting with A on the next row, as shown in figure 18.

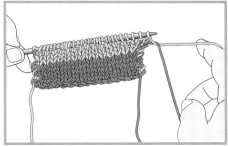

figure 18

This is particularly important when one color is being used on one side of an entire row and another color on the other—a separation will form between the two sides of the knitted fabric unless the yarns are twisted to seal the edges.

FIXING DOUBLE-KNITTING MISTAKES

It's tricky to repair double-sided knitted fabric, but you can do it with a crochet hook. Isolate the stitch that needs to be fixed—usually a stitch that was knitted in the wrong color. Bring your knitting to the column of stitches that includes the mistake. Carefully unravel one side of the knitting down to the offending stitch, correct the error, and use a crochet hook to replace the stitches in the proper order. If necessary, turn the work around and unravel the other side, using the crochet hook to reknit the stitches and replace them in the proper order. For example, in figure 19, a stitch that was originally knitted in yarn A was unraveled and knitted instead in yarn B with the crochet hook. Tug on the yarn to even out the tension and prevent the stitch from appearing uneven. Also make sure the second unused yarn is hidden between the two layers.

figure 19

Casting On and Binding Off for Double Knitting

Because you're essentially knitting two pieces of fabric at the same time, double knitting requires twice as many stitches as regular knitting to achieve the same width. There are several options for casting on for double knitting.

METHOD 1

Using two strands, cast on as usual. On the next row, knit into one of the cast-on strands and purl into the second of the cast-on strands.

METHOD 2

Using one strand, cast on twice as many stitches as you would for ordinary knitting. Begin double knitting on the first row, knitting into the first stitch and purling into the second stitch.

METHOD 3

Using one strand, cast on the same number of stitches that you would for ordinary knitting. On the next row, knit one A and purl one B into each stitch in order to double the number of stitches. This is particularly useful when you want to incorporate some double knitting rows in the middle of a knitted piece that doesn't use double knitting (see the Southport Shawl on page 107).

Binding off can be done in rib pattern if cast-on methods 2 or 3 are used. If casting on with method 1, which will require a tighter bind-off for the bottom and top edges to match, place the knit stitches onto needle 1 and the purl stitches onto needle 2, and use a third needle for the three-needle bind off (see page 19).

Decreasing in Double Knitting

To decrease stitches in double-knit fabric, whether the slip stitch or two-strand method is used, you'll need to reorder the stitches. Two knit stitches must be worked together to make one stitch, and two purl stitches must be worked together to make one stitch. First slip one knit stitch purlwise from the left needle to the right needle. Transfer the next (purl) stitch to a cable needle and hold it in back. Slip the next knit stitch purlwise from the left needle to the right needle. Return the purl stitch from the cable needle to the left needle, then transfer the two slipped stitches on the right needle back to the left needle. You can now decrease the first two knit stitches that have been reordered as well as the following two purl stitches, to ensure that decreases are even on both sides of the fabric. Note that if the slip stitch is used, you'll treat the two purl stitches as though they were one and slip them together with the yarn in front on the first row, and on the return row you'll decrease the two purl stitches in the regular manner. Using this reordering method, you can decrease more than one stitch at a time by reordering the stitches one more time so you'll have three knit followed by three purl stitches at the point when the decrease is specified.

Multidirectional Modular Knitting

In traditional modular knitting, when a shape is created and bound off and new stitches are picked up to add another shape, a seam is created on one side of the work, giving the work a right side and a wrong side. By contrast, the modular projects in this book use reversible knitting to leave no wrong side. They are knit continuously with short rows and use seamless modular construction techniques to join one shape to another (see page 114).

Here are some basic hints for these multidirectional projects.

Casting On

It's important to cast on loosely when knitting on the diagonal. Use a standard long-tail cast-on (see page 17), but instead of casting on with a single needle, cast on with two needles held together. This will double the size of each cast-on stitch and give all of the stitches even tension. After you have cast on the required number of stitches, gently slide one of the needles out of the stitches and begin the project. If the cast-on row is too loose and loopy for your liking, experiment by using a smaller needle with your cast-on needle.

Identifying Decrease Points

In many of these projects, after a decrease instruction you'll turn the work and knit in the other direction, even though the entire row hasn't been knitted. This will result in a hole, or gap, formed at the turning point. The instructions tell you to use a marker to easily find the next decrease point. But once a gap has been formed, you can visually find the decrease point by observing that the first stitch of the decrease (e.g., ssk) is the stitch before the gap, and the second stitch of the decrease is the stitch after the gap—the decrease serves to close the gap. Every time the work is turned a new gap is formed, and an additional stitch from the original group will be used up (see figure 20).

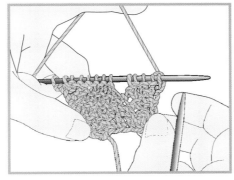

figure 20

Identifying Increase Points

Always double-check the marker that identifies where you'll increase in the center of your work. The stitch in which you increase is the first of that two-stitch pair that was created from the previous row's increase. That stitch has a purl bump on the reverse side. Look for it, and ensure that you're always increasing in the correct place. Figure 21 shows the back side of the newly created stitch that you will increase into on the next row—it's the first stitch on the right needle.

figure 21

Ready to Knit— Both Sides Now

The tips and techniques on the previous pages (along with the abbreviations and terms on the following page) should be enough to get you going into the new world of reversible knits. Your next three steps from here are:

1. Pick a project you'd love to make from the six chapters that follow. I strongly recommend you choose one labeled Beginner or Easy to start.

2. Become familiar with any patterns or stitches relevant to the project, as shown and explained in the Techniques section that begins each chapter.

3. Buy some fabulous yarn, and start your needles!

24

ABBREVIATIONS, TERMS, & STITCH
GLOSSARY

bind off (BO). Knit a stitch, then knit the next stitch and pass the first knitted stitch over the second knitted stitch (a decrease of one stitch); also called cast off.

cast on (CO). When no special cast-on method is specified, use a long-tail cast-on. Make a slip knot in your working yarn, leaving sufficient yarn for the number of cast-on stitches specified by the pattern, and work your way back toward the end as you form the stitches—the extra tail used in this method is the "long tail."

cn. Cable needle.

dpn(s). Double-pointed needle(s).

Garter stitch. Knit every row when working back and forth; knit one row, purl one row when working in the round.

inc1. Knit into the front loop, then into the back loop of the same stitch (one stitch increased).

k1 tbl. Knit one stitch through the back loop.

k1 tfl. Knit one stitch through the front loop.

k2tog. Knit two stitches together as if they were one (one stitch decreased).

long stitch. Knit one stitch, wrapping the yarn two times around the needle to form two loops. On the following row, knit into the first loop of the double wrap and drop the second loop to form an elongated stitch.

M. Marker.

M1. Make one increase. Lift the bar between the stitch on the right needle and the stitch on the left needle, place it on the left needle, and knit into it, making a new stitch.

p2tog. Purl two stitches together as if they were one (one stitch decreased).

PM. Place a marker on the needle.

psso. Pass a slipped stitch over the last worked stitch (one stitch decreased).

Repeat from *. Repeat instructions following the asterisk as many times as indicated.

rm. Remove the marker.

round. A continuous row worked around on circular or double-pointed needles.

short rows. Partial row is worked, then the piece is turned and worked back toward the original edge.

skp. Slip, knit, pass. Slip one stitch knitwise, knit the next stitch, then pass the slipped stitch over the knitted stitch (one stitch decreased).

sl 1b. Slip one stitch with yarn held in back of the work.

sl 1f. Slip one stitch with yarn held in front of the work.

sl 2b. Slip two stitches with yarn in back.

sm. Slip the marker.

ssk. Slip, slip, knit. Slip one stitch, then another stitch knitwise to the right needle, insert the left needle into the fronts of these stitches from left to right, and knit them together (one stitch decreased).

Stockinette stitch. Knit on right-side rows, purl on wrong-side rows when working back and forth; knit all rows when working in the round.

st(s). Stitch(es).

tbl. Through the back loop.

tfl. Through the front loop.

tog. Together.

turn. Transfer the left needle to the right hand and the right needle to the left hand, bringing the yarn up and over to the back between the tops of the two needles.

wyib. With yarn in back of the work.

wyif. With yarn in front of the work.

yarn over (YO). Bring yarn forward under the right needle tip. Wrap it front to back over the needle to form a loop over the needle, adding one stitch. On the following row, work this added loop as a stitch.

One-Yarn Knit/Purl

MANY PATTERNS THAT USE JUST ONE YARN ARE DESIGNED WITH A PUBLIC (RIGHT) SIDE AND A PRIVATE (WRONG) SIDE. CURLING CAN BE A MAJOR PROBLEM WITH PIECES KNITTED FROM A SINGLE YARN, AND HERE YOU'LL LEARN HOW TO PREVENT THAT. YOU'LL ALSO LEARN TO CREATE ONE-YARN PIECES THAT ARE DIFFERENT ON BOTH SIDES. ANY EXERCISE OR COMBINATION OF EXERCISES PRESENTED HERE CAN BE USED TO MAKE TERRIFIC AND EASY REVERSIBLE SCARVES, SHAWLS, OR BLANKETS.

**PROJECTS
IN THIS CHAPTER**

*Brooklyn Hipster Scarf
(left)*

*Sparkle Headband
(back)*

*French Cap
(right)*

ONE-YARN KNIT/PURL
TECHNIQUES

To obtain a similar pattern on each side and ensure that knitted fabric lies flat without curling, choose a pattern that includes approximately equal numbers of knit and purl stitches in every row. Some examples are Garter, Rib, or Seed Stitch Patterns. If curling is a feature of the design (as in the Brooklyn Hipster Scarf on page 31), use an equal number of Stockinette and Reverse Stockinette rows to ensure that the piece is similar on both sides. These are just a few examples of how you can adapt a multitude of different stitch patterns that appear in various stitch guides to make them reversible.

Garter Stitch Pattern

Cast on any number of stitches.

Knit every row.

Since the back of the knit stitch is the purl stitch, the Garter Stitch Pattern will never curl. Each side of the piece has one knit row followed by one purl row, and there are an equal number of knit and purl stitches on each side. ■

Stockinette and Reverse Stockinette Pattern

Cast on any number of stitches.

Row 1: Knit.

Row 2: Purl.

Row 3: Knit.

Row 4: Knit.

Row 5: Purl.

Row 6: Knit.

Repeat rows 1–6 for pattern.

In Stockinette stitch, where one row is knitted and the next row is purled, the knitted fabric will always curl. Accompany Stockinette (rows 1–3) with Reverse Stockinette (rows 4–6), and the knitted piece curls evenly first in one direction and then in the other. ■

<table>
<tr><td>

Cast on an odd number of stitches.

Row 1: *K1, p1; repeat from * to last st, k1.

Row 2: *P1, k1; repeat from * to last st, p1.

Repeat rows 1 and 2 for pattern.

Alternate knit and purl stitches on one side, and the resulting fabric will not curl. Then on the other side, work every knit and purl as they face you to create vertical ridges in the knitting. Because the fabric pulls in like an accordion, the 1x1 Rib Pattern looks like Stockinette fabric on both sides—the purl stitches are hidden between the knits. This pattern is used extensively in the double knitting techniques presented in the later chapters.

To get a different pattern on each side, you can vary the 1x1 Rib Pattern with an uneven ratio of knit to purl stitches, as seen in the Uneven Rib Pattern on page 30. You can also use hidden purl stitches in the rib fabric to add interesting details. ■

</td><td>

Cast on in multiples of 2 stitches.

Row 1: *K1 tbl, p1; repeat from * to end of row.

Row 2: *P1 tbl, k1; repeat from * to end of row.

Repeat rows 1 and 2 for pattern.

Using this interesting "twist" on the simple Rib Pattern creates a different-looking rib on each side, even though the number of knit and purl stitches in the rib are the same. ■

</td><td>

Cast on in multiples of 5 stitches.

Row 1: *K3, p2; repeat from * to end of row.

Row 2: *K2, p3; repeat from * to end of row.

Row 3: *Bring yarn to front, sl 3, bring yarn to back, return 3 sts just slipped to left needle, k3 (all 3 stitches are now wrapped), p2; repeat from * to end of row.

Row 4: Repeat row 2.

Repeat rows 1–4 for pattern.

This pattern works a design into the knit stitches on one side of the fabric, which will be hidden in the purl stitches of the other side of the fabric. ■

</td></tr>
</table>

Uneven Rib Pattern (1x3 Rib)

Cluster Pattern (2x3 Rib)

Cast on in multiples of 4 plus 3 stitches.

Row 1: K1, *k1, p3; repeat from * to last 2 sts, k2.

Row 2: K1, *p1, k3; repeat from * to last 2 sts, p1, k1.

Repeat rows 1 and 2 for pattern.

Combinations like 1x2 (1 knit, 2 purl), 1x3 (1 knit, 3 purl), 2x3 (2 knit, 3 purl) result in a fabric that is different on each side. Although there are more or fewer knit stitches than purl stitches on one side, and more or fewer purl stitches than knit stitches on the other side, the fabric will usually not curl. Maintain a reasonable ratio to ensure this (such as not exceeding a 1 to 5 ratio of knit to purl stitches). Always test out the fabric, since all yarns are different. To maintain symmetry, end with a final repeat of the first number in the rib stitch ratio. For example, in a 1x3 rib stitch pattern, which is k1, p3, end with a k1. ▪

Cast on in multiples of 5 stitches.

Rows 1 and 3: *K2, p3; repeat from * to end of row.

Row 2: *K1, [k1, yo, k1] into next st, turn, p3, turn, sl 1, k2tog, psso, k1, p2; repeat from * to end of row.

Row 4: *K3, p2; repeat from * to end of row.

Repeat rows 1–4 for pattern.

This example shows how to work a design in the center knit stitch of the rib pattern on one side, which will be hidden in the purl stitch of the rib pattern on the other side. ▪

30

Brooklyn Hipster Scarf

Skill Level
● ● ● ●
Beginner

TECHNIQUE
*Stockinette and
Reverse Stockinette Pattern
(page 28)*

31

LONGING LOOKS FOREVER

Finished Measurements

4"/10cm wide x 26"/66cm long in unstretched pattern stitch

Materials

Yarn: 104yd/95m of (4) medium weight wool, in green

Knitting needles: 4.5 mm (size 7 U.S.) *or size to obtain gauge*

2 buttons, ¾"/2cm wide

Yarn needle

Gauge

16 stitches and 23 rows = 4"/10cm in Stockinette stitch

Always take time to check your gauge.

Special Stitches

Stockinette (see page 28).

Reverse Stockinette (see page 28).

Pattern

Alternate 7 rows in Stockinette with 7 rows in Reverse Stockinette.

Instructions

SETUP

CO 3 sts.

Row 1: Inc1, work in pattern to last st, p1.

Repeat row 1 until there are 29 sts on needles.

BODY

Row 1: Inc1, work in pattern to last 2 sts, p2tog.

Row 2: Work in pattern to last st, p1.

Repeat rows 1–2 until piece measures 25"/64cm (on long edge).

32

Brooklyn Hipster Scarf

END

Row 1: Work in pattern to last 2 sts, p2tog.

Repeat row 1 until there are 3 sts, then sl 1, k2tog, psso.

FINISHING

Cut yarn, weave in ends. Sew buttons at one end (top and bottom), spaced about 3"/8cm apart. It is not necessary to make buttonholes—the yarn is stretchy enough to create buttonholes and accommodate buttons as needed, leaving you the flexibility to fasten it in various ways depending on your outerwear.

This project was knit with:

Artyarns Supermerino, 100% merino wool, 1¾ oz/50g = 104yd/95m per skein, 1 skein color #283. To find equivalent yarn brands from other makers, see the Yarn Substitution Chart on page 142.

Sparkle Headband

Skill Level
● ● ● ●
Beginner

TECHNIQUE
*Twisted Rib Pattern
(page 29)*

34

FRESH + FLIRTY

Finished Measurements

18"/46cm in circumference x 2"/5cm wide

Materials

Yarn: 80yd/73m of 〔3〕 light weight yarn, embellished mohair-and-silk blend, in tweed multicolor

Knitting needles: 3.0 mm (size 3 U.S.) circular needle 16"/40cm long *or size to obtain gauge*

Stitch marker

Gauge

28 stitches and 36 rows = 4"/10cm in Twisted Rib Pattern

Always take time to check your gauge.

Pattern

Twisted Rib Pattern (see page 29):

Round 1: *K1 tbl, p1; repeat from * to end of round.

Repeat round 1 for pattern.

Instructions

CO 126 sts and join to knit in the round. Place marker to identify start of round.

Rounds 1–20: Work Twisted Rib Pattern, slipping marker.

Bind off in pattern as follows: K1 tbl, p1, bind off, *k1 tbl, bind off, p1, bind off; repeat from * until 1 st remains. Cut yarn and pull through remaining stitch. Weave in ends.

This project was knit with:
Artyarns Beaded Mohair & Sequins, 80% silk with glass beads, 20% kid mohair, 1¾ oz/50g = 114yd/104m per skein, 1 skein color #112. To find equivalent yarn brands from other makers, see the Yarn Substitution Chart on page 142.

French Cap

Skill Level

● ● ● ●

Easy

TECHNIQUES
Garter Stitch Pattern
(page 28)

Rib Pattern and Bar Pattern
(page 29)

Uneven Rib Pattern
and Cluster Pattern
(page 30)

36

CAFÉ SOCIETY

Finished Measurements

18"/46cm in circumference x 7"/18cm deep

Materials

Yarn: 104yd/95m of (4) medium weight yarn, wool, in teal

Knitting needles: 4.5 mm (size 7 U.S.) circular 16"/40cm knitting needles *or size to obtain gauge*

Stitch markers

Yarn needle

Gauge

16 stitches and 32 rows = 4"/10cm in Garter stitch

Always take time to check your gauge.

Special Stitches

Cluster Stitch (CS): [k1, yo, k1] into the same stitch, turn; p3, turn; sl 1b, k2tog, psso (see page 30).

Bar Stitch: Sl 3f, bring yarn to back, sl 3 from right back to left needle, k3 (yarn has wrapped around stitches). See page 29.

Patterns

Circular Garter Pattern (see page 28):

Round 1: Knit.

Round 2: Purl.

Repeat rounds 1 and 2 for pattern.

Note: Work on circular needles and switch to dpns when there are too few stitches remaining on the circular needle for comfortable knitting.

Instructions

CO 48 sts. Place a marker and join to work in the round.

Rounds 1–4: *K1, p1; repeat from * to end of round—48 sts.

Round 5: K1, inc1; repeat from * to end of round—72 sts.

Round 6: *K3, p3; repeat from * to end of round (12 repeats).

Round 7: *[K1, CS, k1], p3, Bar Stitch, p3; repeat from * to end of round (6 repeats).

Round 8: *[CS, k1, CS], p3, Bar Stitch, p3; repeat from * to end of round (6 repeats).

French Cap

Round 9: Repeat round 7.

Rounds 10–12: *Bar Stitch, p3, k3, p3; repeat from * to end of round (6 repeats).

Round 13: *K3, p3, [k1, CS, k1], p3; repeat from * to end of round (6 repeats).

Round 14: *K3, p3, [CS, k1, CS], p3; repeat from * to end of round (6 repeats).

Round 15: Repeat round 13.

Work 6 rounds in Circular Garter Pattern, inserting stitch markers after every 12 sts on round 6.

DECREASE TOP

Round 1: *K to 2 sts before marker, ssk, sm; repeat from * to end of round—6 sts decreased.

Round 2: Purl.

Repeat rounds 1 and 2 until 6 sts remain.

FINISHING

Cut yarn, thread tail onto yarn needle, draw through remaining 6 sts, and pull tightly. Fasten off, weave in ends.

This project was knit with:
Artyarns Supermerino, 100% merino wool, $1\frac{3}{4}$ oz/50g = 104yd/95m per skein, 1 skein color #279. To find equivalent yarn brands from other makers, see the Yarn Substitution Chart on page 142.

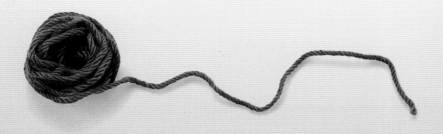

Multi-Yarn Knit/Purl

THIS CHAPTER COVERS REVERSIBLE KNITTING IN TWO OR MORE YARNS IN TWO OR MORE COLORS. WHEN CHANGING COLORS IN STRAIGHT GARTER OR STOCKINETTE STITCH, WHETHER YOU'RE WORKING IN HORIZONTAL STRIPES OR CHANGING COLOR IN THE MIDDLE OF A ROW, THE COLOR CHANGE IS USUALLY VERY OBVIOUS ON ONE SIDE OF THE WORK. HERE YOU'LL FIND SOME IDEAS AND TECHNIQUES THAT MAKE SUCH ABRUPT CHANGES MORE SUBTLE, AS WELL AS SOME IDEAS FOR DISGUISING THEM ALTOGETHER.

PROJECTS IN THIS CHAPTER

Asphalt Ascot (left)

Sawtooth Scarf (right)

Riff Belt

Nordic Tracks Hoodie

MULTI-YARN KNIT/PURL TECHNIQUES

Some of the techniques presented here will produce the same pattern on both sides, while others result in two sides that are startlingly different from each other.

Working with two yarns in two or more colors is a major challenge for those trying to create two right sides. These pages present some solutions to this problem, ranging from circular knitting to simple slip stitches.

Using decreases at the color-change point in the middle of a row will disguise the change and produce a smooth transition as shown at left. Changing colors without decreases causes interrupting bumps at the transition as shown below.

Make sure to twist the yarns around each other when changing colors, to prevent holes from forming. ■

Note: Slip sts pwise with yarn in back.

Setup: With color A, CO 10 sts. Slide sts to other side of needle. With color B, CO 10 additional sts in front of the A sts.

Row 1: With B, k9, ssk, turn, sl 1, M1, k to end of row; slide sts to other end of needle.

Row 2: With A, k8, ssk, turn, sl 1, M1, k to end of row; slide sts to other end of needle.

Repeat rows 1 and 2 for pattern.

Two-Color 1x1 Rib Pattern

Cast on 21 sts with color A.

Row 1: With A, *k1, p1; repeat from * to last st, k1.

Row 2: With A, *p1, k1; repeat from * to last st, p1. Drop A, attach B.

Row 3: With B, *k1, p1; repeat from * to last st, k1.

Row 4: With B, *p1, k1; repeat from * to last st, p1. Drop B, attach A.

Repeat rows 1–4 for pattern.

Page 15 shows how to carry yarns along sides when changing colors. Changing color in Rib Pattern will result in a smooth transition between two colors. When working horizontal stripes in 1x1 Rib Pattern, the purl stitches are hidden between the knit stitches, so the color-change bumps don't show, making a smooth transition between the colors. ∎

Circular Stockinette Pattern

Using small circular needle (16"/40cm length), CO 40 sts. Join to work in the round (see page 14), and place marker to identify the start of the round.

Rounds 1 and 2: With A, knit. Drop A, attach B.

Rounds 3 and 4: With B, knit. Drop B, attach A.

Repeat rounds 1–4 for pattern, slipping markers.

Circular knitting is one way to achieve knitted fabric that is the same on both sides. The openings at the bottom and top can be seamed, or if you use the provisional cast-on (see page 17), you can seal the top and bottom of the piece with a 3-needle bind-off (see page 19). I recommend this technique only for soft and/or fine yarns; heavy yarns will produce unsightly, bulky knits. ∎

Slip Stitch Pattern with Exposed Weaving

With A, CO a multiple of 4 plus 3 stitches.

Row 1: With A, *k1, p1; repeat from * to last st, k1.

Row 2: With A, k2, *p1, k1; repeat from *. Drop A, attach B.

Row 3: With B, k1, p1, *sl 3b, p1; repeat from * to last st, k1.

Row 4: With B, k2, *sl 3f, k1; repeat from *. Drop B, attach A.

Repeat rows 1–4 for pattern.

Each side of the knitted fabric will appear different. On one side the color of the exposed weaving will be emphasized, while it will not show at all on the other side. The purl stitches are completely hidden in the 1x1 Rib Pattern, and the slipped stitches appear extra long because they are carried up for 2 extra rows without being knitted. The concept will be explored further in the Double Knitting chapter. ■

Asphalt
Ascot

Skill Level
● ● ● ●
Intermediate

TECHNIQUE
Decreased Color Change Pattern
(page 42)

TREAD LIGHTLY

Finished Measurements

6½"/17cm wide x 50"/127cm long

Materials

Yarn: 573yd/525m of (1) super fine yarn, wool, in three variegated colors

• Color A: 191yd/175m, in navy, brown, and beige

• Color B: 191yd/175m, in black, gray, and cream

• Color C: 191yd/175m, in olive and pale gray-blue

Knitting needles: 3.75 mm (size 5 U.S.) *or size to obtain gauge*

Stitch markers

Stitch holders

Gauge

20 stitches and 40 rows = 4"/10cm in Garter stitch

Always take time to check your gauge.

Instructions

SETUP

With Color A, CO 3 sts.

Row 1: K1, inc1, p1.

Row 2: Inc1, inc1, pm, k1, p1.

Row 3: Inc1, k to marker, rm, inc1, pm, k to last st, p1.

Repeat row 3 until you have 14 sts. Leave working yarn attached and transfer the stitches to a stitch holder. One panel formed.

Repeat the setup with Color B, and repeat it again with Color C to create two additional panels.

ATTACHING THE PANELS

Holding a needle pointing from left to right, place all three panels on the needle with working yarn attached to the stitch on the right of each panel as it is transferred from the stitch holder. Place them in the

following order: Color C panel, followed by Color B panel, followed by Color A panel, which is the first panel ready to be knitted.

KNITTING IT ALL TOGETHER

Note: When changing colors, drop the old color in front and work with the new color. On the return row, bring the strand to the back of the work to continue.

Row 1: With A, k6, inc1, k6, k2tog, drop A, and wrap B up from behind and around A to continue knitting; with B, k5, inc1, k6, k2tog, drop B, and wrap C up from behind and around B to continue knitting; with C, k5, inc1, k5, k2tog.

Row 2: With C, k6, inc1, k5, k2tog; with B, k6, inc1, k5, k2tog; with A, k6, inc1, k5, k2tog.

Repeat rows 1 and 2 until scarf is 50"/127cm long or yarn is nearly used up. Bind off all stitches in kind (use color A to bind off A, color B to bind off B, and color C to bind off C). Cut yarn. Weave in ends.

This project was knit with:
Artyarns Ultramerino 4, 100% merino wool, 1¾oz/50g = 191yd/175m per skein, 1 skein each colors A: 143, B: 117, C: 159. To find equivalent yarn brands from other makers, see the Yarn Substitution Chart on page 142.

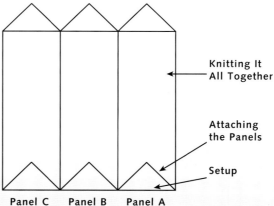

Knitting It
All Together

Attaching
the Panels

Setup

Panel C   Panel B   Panel A

Sawtooth Scarf

Skill Level
• • • •
Intermediate

TECHNIQUE
*Decreased Color
Change Pattern
(page 42)*

DANGEROUSLY CHIC

Finished Measurements

Approximately 5"/13cm wide x 51"/130cm long

Materials

Yarn: 416yd/380m of (4) medium weight yarn, wool, in two colors

- Color A: 208yd/190m, in coral

- Color B: 208yd/190m, in deep burgundy

Knitting needles: 5 mm (size 8 U.S.) 24"/40cm circular *or size to obtain gauge*

Stitch marker

Yarn needle

Gauge

16 stitches and 32 rows = 4"/10cm in Garter stitch

Always take time to check your gauge.

Instructions

SETUP

With A, CO 8 sts.

Row 1: Inc1, k1, turn; sl 1b, k to last st, p1. Note: A gap will form between the slipped stitch and the remaining cast-on stitches.

Row 2: Inc1, k to gap, k1, turn; sl 1b, k to last st, p1.

Repeat row 2 until you have 15 sts. Drop A. Slide sts to opposite end of needle.

Sawtooth Scarf

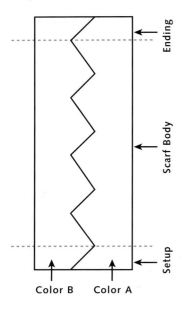

Color B   Color A

With B, on the same needle but at other end of the A working yarn, CO 10 sts.

Row 1: With B, inc1, k1, turn; sl 1b, k to last st, p1.

Row 2: With B, inc1, k to gap, k1, turn; sl 1b, k to last st, p1.

Repeat row 2 until you have 19 sts. Drop B.

SCARF BODY

Slide sts to the other end of the needle so you're ready to work with A.

Row 1: With A, inc1, k to last st of A, ssk (1 st of A and 1 st of B); turn; sl 1b, k to last st, p1.

Repeat row 1 until 14 sts of B remain.

Slide sts to the other end of the needle so you're ready to work with B.

Row 1: With B, inc1, k to last st of B, ssk (1 st of A and 1 st of B); turn; sl 1b, k to last st, p1.

Repeat row 1 until 14 sts of A remain.

Slide sts to the other end of the needle so you're ready to work with A.

Continue in this manner until scarf measures 47"/119cm or 4"/10cm less than desired finished length.

SCARF ENDING

With A:

Row 1: Inc1, k12, ssk, turn; sl 1b, k13, p1.

Row 2: Inc1, k13, ssk, turn; sl 1b, k14, p1.

Row 3: Inc1, k14, ssk, turn; sl 1b, k14, p2tog.

Row 4: Sl 1b, k14, ssk, turn; sl 1b, k13, p2tog.

Slide stitches to other side of needle.

With B:

Row 1: Sl 1b, k13, ssk, turn; sl 1b, k12, p2tog.

Row 2: Sl 1b, k12, ssk, turn; sl 1b, k11, p2tog.

Row 3: Sl 1b, k11, ssk, turn; sl 1b, k10, p2tog.

Row 4: Sl 1b, k10, ssk, turn; sl 1b, k9, p2tog.

Slide stitches to other side of needle.

With A:

Row 1: Sl 1b, k9, ssk, turn; sl 1b, k8, p2tog.

Row 2: Sl 1b, k8, ssk, turn; sl 1b, k7, p2tog.

Row 3: Sl 1b, k7, ssk, turn; sl 1b, k6, p2tog.

Row 4: Sl 1b, k6, ssk, turn; sl 1b, k5, p2tog.

Slide stitches to other side of needle.

With B:

Row 1: Sl 1b, k5, ssk, turn; sl 1b, k4, p2tog.

Row 2: Sl 1b, k4, ssk, turn; sl 1b, k3, p2tog.

Row 3: Sl 1b, k3, ssk, turn; sl 1b, k2, p2tog.

Row 4: Sl 1b, k2, ssk, turn; sl 1b, k1, p2tog.

Slide stitches to other side of needle.

With A:

Row 1: Sl 1b, k1, ssk, turn; sl 1b, p2tog.

Row 2: Sl 1b, ssk, k1, turn; sl 1b, k2tog, psso.

Cut yarn. Pass through last stitch to bind off. Weave in ends.

This project was knit with:
Artyarns Supermerino, 100% merino wool, 1¾ oz/50g = 104yd/95m per skein, 2 skeins color #254, and 2 skeins color #256. To find equivalent yarn brands from other makers, see the Yarn Substitution Chart on page 142.

Riff Belt

Skill Level
● ● ● ●
Intermediate

TECHNIQUES
Two-Color 1x1 Rib Pattern
(page 43)

and Slip Stitch Pattern
with Exposed Weaving
(page 44)

LATENIGHT GIG

Note: I adapted the stitch pattern from Barbara Walker's Quilted Lattice pattern in *A Treasury of Knitting Patterns*.

Finished Measurements

3"/8 wide x 31"/79m long

Materials

Yarn: 340yd/311m of (3) light weight yarn, silk, in two colors

- Color A: 170yd/155m, in brown
- Color B: 170yd/155m, in salmon

Knitting needles: 2.75 mm (size 2 U.S.) double-pointed needles (3) *or size to obtain gauge*

Standard 3" round brass or gold-plated belt ring with center bar and prong

Yarn needle

Gauge

24 stitches and 24 rows = 4"/10cm in pattern stitch

Always take time to check your gauge.

Special Stitch

Pickup-k1: Place the point of the right needle under the 2 loose strands of contrasting color from front to back, then knit the next stitch.

Pattern

Rib Pattern (see page 43):

Row 1 and all odd-numbered rows: *K1, p1; repeat to last st, k1.

Row 2 and all even-numbered rows: K1, *k1, p1; repeat to last 2 sts, k2.

Instructions

KNIT THE BUCKLE END

Follow the instructions for Casting on to a Belt Ring on page 18, casting on 18 sts and knitting 4 rows. Continue with the instructions, ending with 36 stitches. Now you'll use two needles again.

Row 1: Inc1, *k1, p1; repeat from * 9 times, inc1, *k1, p1; repeat from * to last 2 sts, k1, inc1—39 sts.

At this point all stitches are now firmly attached to the buckle. The first few rows may be awkward.

Rows 2–6: With A, work in Rib Pattern over 6 rows.

Riff Belt

Row 7: Attach B. With B, k1, p1, [sl 11b, p1] 3 times, k1—39 sts.

Row 8: With B, k2, [sl 11f, k1] 3 times, k1, drop B.

Row 9: With A, work in Rib Pattern.

Row 10: With A, k1, [k1, p1] 3 times, [pickup-k1, p1, (k1, p1) 5 times] twice, pickup-k1, p1, [k1, p1] twice, k2, drop A.

Row 11: With B, k1, p1, sl 5b, p1, [sl 11b, p1] twice, sl 5b, p1, k1.

Row 12: With B, k2, sl 5f, k1, [sl11f, k1] twice, sl 5f, k2, drop B.

Row 13: With A, work in Rib Pattern.

Row 14: With A, k1, [k1, p1] 6 times, [pickup-k1, p1, (k1, p1) 5 times] twice, k2.

Rows 15 and 16: With A, work in Rib Pattern.

KNIT THE BELT BODY

Rows 1 and 2: With B, work in Rib Pattern. (This should be 2 rows of rib—the next row is an odd-numbered pattern row.)

Row 3: With A, k1, p1, [sl 11b, p1] 3 times, k1—39 sts.

Row 4: With A, k2, [sl 11f, k1] 3 times, k1, drop A.

Row 5: With B, work in Rib Pattern.

Row 6: With B, k1, [k1, p1] 3 times, [Pickup-k1, p1, (k1, p1) 5 times] twice, pickup-k1, p1, [k1, p1] twice, k2, drop B.

Row 7: With A, k1, p1, sl 5b, p1, [sl 11b, p1] twice, sl 5b, p1, k1.

Row 8: With A, k2, sl 5f k1, [sl 11f, k1] twice, sl 5f, k2, drop A.

Row 9: With B, work in Rib Pattern.

Row 10: With B, k1, [k1, p1] 6 times, [pickup-k1, p1, (k1, p1) 5 times] twice, k2.

Repeat Rows 3–10 until belt measures 26"/66cm.

KNIT THE BELT END

Switch colors again by repeating rows 9–14 of the Buckle End until belt measures 31"/79cm. Bind off by transferring all knit stitches to needle 1, transferring all purl stitches to needle 2, and using a third needle to work a 3-needle bind-off (see page 19).

FINISHING

Cut yarn, weave in ends. To make a belt loop, with B, provisionally CO 4 sts.

Row 1: K1, p1; repeat from *.

Repeat row 1 until loop measures 6"/15cm. Transfer provisional CO sts to second needle. Using 3-needle bind-off, bind off all sts together. Cut yarn. Weave in ends. Slip loop onto belt.

This project was knit with:
Artyarns Silk Pearl, 100% silk, 1¾oz/50g = 170yd/155m per skein, 1 skein color #268, 1 skein color #2281. To find equivalent yarn brands from other makers, see the Yarn Substitution Chart on page 142.

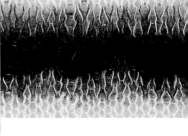

Nordic
Tracks
Hoodie

Skill Level
• • • •
Intermediate

TECHNIQUE
Circular Stockinette Pattern
(page 43)

BUNDLE UP

Finished Measurements

10"/25cm wide x 74"/188cm long

Materials

Yarn: 600yd/549m of  lace weight yarn, mohair-and-silk blend, 100yd/91m in each of six colors, A: black, B: yellow, C: cream, D: blue, E: pale beige, F: dark beige

Knitting needles: 4.0 mm (size 6 U.S.) 16"/40cm circular *or size to obtain gauge*; 4 mm (size 6 U.S.) double-pointed needles for 3-needle bind-off.

Stitch marker

Stitch holder

Tapestry needle

Gauge

18 stitches and 22 rows = 4"/10cm in Stockinette stitch

Always take the time to check your gauge.

Note: Two strands of yarn are held throughout. Although turning is used, you will not need to wrap any stitches.

Pattern

Short Row Pattern:

Row 1: *K3, turn, k3, turn, k6; repeat from * to end of round.

Instructions

With 2 strands of A, circular needle, and using the provisional cast-on (see page 17), CO 80 sts. Join and place marker to identify start of round.

Rounds 1–3: Knit.

Round 4: Work Short Row Pattern.

Rounds 5–7: Knit.

Blend by cutting 1 strand of A and adding 1 strand of B. Knit 2 rounds. Cut 1 strand of A and add another strand of B. With B, knit 3 rounds. Cut 1 strand of B and add 1 strand of C. Knit 2 rounds. Cut 1 strand of B and add 1 strand of C. With C, knit 3 rounds. Cut 1 strand of C and add 1 strand of A. Knit 2 rounds. Cut 1 strand of C and add 1 strand of A. With 2 strands of A, knit.

Repeat instructions for rounds 2–7. Then work colors in the following order:

AB 2 rounds, BB 3 rounds, BC 2 rounds, CC 3 rounds, CA 2 rounds.

AA 3 rounds knit, 1 round Short Row Pattern, 3 rounds knit.

AD 2 rounds, DD 3 rounds, DE 2 rounds, EE 3 rounds, EA 2 rounds.

AA 3 rounds knit, 1 round Short Row Pattern, 3 rounds knit.

AF 2 rounds, FF 3 rounds, FB 2 rounds, BB 3 rounds, BA 2 rounds.

AA 3 rounds knit, 1 round Short Row Pattern, 3 rounds knit.

AC 2 rounds, CC 3 rounds, CD 2 rounds, DD 3 rounds, DA 2 rounds.

AA 3 rounds knit, 1 round Short Row Pattern, 3 rounds knit.

AE 2 rounds, EE 3 rounds, EF 2 rounds, FF 3 rounds, FA 2 rounds.

AA 3 rounds knit, 1 round Short Row Pattern, 3 rounds knit.

Repeat from this color sequence until scarf measures 74"/188cm. Transfer an equal number of stitches onto each of two needles. Using a third needle and 2 strands of A, bind off with a 3-needle bind-off (see page 19). This seals the bottom of the piece. Repeat at the cast-on edge, by transferring half the provisional cast-on stitches onto one needle, and the corresponding ones to the other. Make sure that the scarf is in alignment and the stitches match up from top to bottom, then bind off with a 3-needle bind-off. Cut yarn, weave in ends.

FINISHING

Thread a tapestry needle with 1 strand of Yarn C. Fold piece exactly in half and seam approximately 10"/25cm from the center back. Fasten off the yarn and weave in the ends.

This project was knit with:
Artyarns Silk Mohair, 60% kid mohair/40% silk, 0.9oz/50g = 312yd/285m per skein; 1 skein in color #246, 1 skein in color #250, 1 skein in color #223, 1 skein in color #2205, 1 skein in color #253, and 1 skein in color #257. To find equivalent yarn brands from other makers, see the Yarn Substitution Chart on page 142.

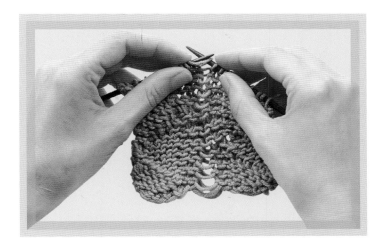

Lace

LACE IS COMPOSED OF EYELETS, OR HOLES, IN KNITTING, AND THESE CAN APPEAR LOVELY ON BOTH SIDES. MOST KNITTED PIECES WHERE APPROXIMATELY HALF THE STITCHES ARE MADE UP OF LACE CAN BE USED COMFORTABLY WITH BOTH SIDES SHOWING, PARTICULARLY WHEN A VERY SOFT YARN IS USED, SUCH AS CASHMERE OR MOHAIR. IF THERE ARE SECTIONS OF KNITTING BETWEEN LACE THAT SERVE TO OFFSET THE LACE, THEY MUST BE IN A PATTERN THAT MAINTAINS AN EVEN COUNT OF KNIT AND PURL STITCHES, TO PREVENT CURLING.

**PROJECTS
IN THIS CHAPTER**

*Sorbet Shawl
(right)*

*La Parisienne Collar
(left)*

LACE TECHNIQUES

In lace patterns where yarn overs are accompanied by corresponding single decreases, the decreases will always slant in a particular direction—either left or right. And they will be either knitted or purled decreases, which means that the stitch appearance on the other side will be the opposite. A slant in one direction on one side will skew the fabric in one direction on one side and the opposite on the other. The position of the eyelet can further affect the degree of skew.

One way to ensure similarity on both sides is to use center double decreases (e.g., sl 2tog, k1, p2sso). Another way is to consider the direction of knit and purl decreases as well as the accompanying stitch pattern. The following examples balance the lace to prevent skewing while also maintaining the balance of knit and purl stitches. There are two types of lace patterns shown—those where eyelets are created in every row (labeled faggoting here), and those where eyelets are created in only every other row (labeled alternating here).

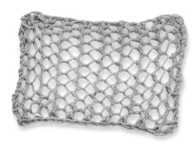

Cast on a multiple of 2 stitches.

Row 1: K1, *yo, skp; repeat from * to last st, k1.

Repeat row 1 for pattern.

Every group of 2 stitches in this simple faggoting pattern is worked the same way—a yarn over is accompanied by a left-leaning decrease. I call this Garter Lace, because the same knitted decrease is used on both sides of the knitted piece. The same effect could be achieved with any type of decrease, even one of the purl decreases (p2tog or p2tog tbl). This is an ideal pattern to work in two or more colors, because the color change is hidden in the decrease, making both sides look the same. An example of this technique is in the Southport Shawl on page 107. ■

Cast on a multiple of 6 plus 5 stitches.

Row 1: K1, *yo, sl 2tog, k1, p2sso, yo, p3; repeat from * to last 4 sts, yo, sl 2tog, k1, p2sso, yo, k1.

Row 2: K1, *p3, k3; repeat from * to last 4 sts, p3, k1.

Repeat rows 1 and 2 for pattern.

This pattern has double eyelets with a center double decrease followed by purl panels, alternating with 3x3 Rib on the other side.

In the Rib stitch, when knit stitches alternate with a complementary number of purl stitches, there is no curling. The center double decrease pattern prevents skewing. A similar effect to the double decrease can be achieved if left- and right-leaning decreases are matched, as shown in the next exercise. ■

Alternating Matched Decrease Pattern

ABBREVIATIONS

LR (Lace Right): k2tog, k1, p1, k1, yo.

LL (Lace Left): yo, k1, p1, k1, skp.

Cast on 25 stitches.

Row 1: K6, LR, p1, k1, p1, LL, k6.

Row 2: K6, [p2, k1] twice, p1, [k1, p2] twice, k6.

Row 3: K5, LR, [k1, p1] twice, k1, LL, k5.

Row 4: K5, p2, k1, p2, [p1, k1] twice, p1, p2, k1, p2, k5.

Row 5: K4, LR, [p1, k1] 3 times, p1, LL, k4.

Row 6: K4, p2, k1, p2, [k1, p1] 3 times, k1, p2, k1, p2, k4.

Row 7: K3, LR, [k1, p1] 4 times, k1, LL, k3.

Row 8: K3, p2, k1, p2, [p1, k1] 4 times, p1, p2, k1, p2, k3.

Repeat rows 1–8 for pattern.

Using both right- and left-leaning decreases balances a pattern, as shown here in this Rib Lace pattern that is different on each side. On one side, a single column of Stockinette stitch angles out from the center, and on the other side three columns angle out. Garter panels form the edging. ▪

Sorbet
Shawl

Skill Level
● ● ● ●
Easy

TECHNIQUE
*Alternating Matched
Decrease Pattern
(page 61)*

EARLY MORNING ALLURE

Finished Measurements

51"/130cm wide x 30"/76cm deep

Materials

Yarn: 760yds/695m of (3) light weight yarn, cashmere and mohair blend, in variegated pinks and browns

Knitting needles: 4 mm (size 6 U.S.) *or size to obtain gauge*

Yarn needle

Gauge

16 stitches and 30 rows = 4"/10cm in Lace Pattern

Always take time to check your gauge.

Patterns

CENTER TRIANGLE STOCKINETTE

Row 1: K2tog, yo, k1, yo, skp.

Row 2 and all even-numbered rows: Purl.

Row 3: K2tog, yo, k3, yo, skp.

Row 5: K2tog, yo, k5, yo, skp.

Row 7: K2tog, yo, k7, yo, skp.

Row 9: K2tog, yo, k9, yo, skp.

Row 11: K2tog, yo, k11, yo, skp.

Row 12: Purl.

CENTER TRIANGLE REVERSE STOCKINETTE

Row 1: K2tog, yo, p1, yo, skp.

Row 2: P2, k1, p2.

Row 3: K2tog, yo, p3, yo, skp.

Row 4: P2, k3, p2.

Row 5: K2tog, yo, p5, yo, skp.

Row 6: P2, k5, p2.

Row 7: K2tog, yo, p7, yo, skp.

Row 8: P2, k7, p2.

Row 9: K2tog, yo, p9, yo, skp.

Row 10: P2, k9, p2.

Row 11: K2tog, yo, p11, yo, skp.

Row 12: P2, k11, p2.

Sorbet Shawl

RIGHT-LEANING STOCKINETTE

Row 1: K2tog, yo, k4.

Row 2: Purl.

RIGHT-LEANING REVERSE STOCKINETTE

Row 1: K2tog, yo, p4.

Row 2: K4, p2.

LEFT-LEANING STOCKINETTE

Row 1: K4, yo, skp.

Row 2: Purl.

LEFT-LEANING REVERSE STOCKINETTE

Row 1: P4, yo, skp.

Row 2: P2, k4.

Instructions

Note: The shawl starts with one center repeat and ends with 33—16 on each side and one in the center. Maintain edge stitches throughout as follows: k1 tbl, yo, work pattern as instructed to last stitch, sl 1f—1 stitch increased per row.

CO 3 sts.

SETUP IN STOCKINETTE

Row 1: K1 tbl, yo, k1, sl 1f—4 sts.

Row 2: K1 tbl, yo, p2, sl 1f—5 sts.

Row 3: K1 tbl, yo, k3, sl 1f—6 sts.

Row 4: K1 tbl, yo, p4, sl 1f—7 sts.

Chart

```
|   |   |   | - | - | - | - |   |   |   |   |   |   |   |   | - |   |   |   |   | - | - | - | - |
| \ | 0 | - | - | - | - | \ | 0 |   |   |   | \ | 0 | - | 0 | / |   |   | 0 | / | - | - | - | - | 0 | / |
|   |   | - | - | - | - |   |   |   |   |   |   |   |   |   |   |   |   | - | - | - | - |
|   | \ | 0 | - | - | - | - | \ | 0 |   |   |   |   |   |   |   |   | 0 | / | - | - | - | - | 0 | / |
|   |   |   | - | - | - | - |   |   |   |   |   |   |   |   |   | - | - | - | - |
|   |   | \ | 0 | - | - | - | - | \ | 0 |   |   |   |   | 0 | / | - | - | - | - | 0 | / |
|   |   |   |   | - | - | - | - |   |   |   |   |   | - | - | - | - |
|   |   |   | \ | 0 | - | - | - | - | \ | 0 |   | 0 | / | - | - | - | - | 0 | / |
|   |   |   |   |   | - | - | - | - |   |   |   | - | - | - | - |
|   |   |   |   | \ | 0 | - | - | - | - | \ | 0 | 0 | / | - | - | - | - | 0 | / |
| 0 |   |   |   |   |   |   | \ | 0 | - | - | - | - | \ | 0 | 0 | / | - | - | - | - | 0 | / |   |   | 0 |
|   |   |   |   |   |   | - | - | - | - |   |   | - | - | - | - |
| \ | 0 |   |   |   |   | \ | 0 | - | - | - | - | \ | 0 | 0 | / | - | - | - | - | 0 | / |   |   | 0 | / |
```

Legend: ☐ Knit on front, purl on back — – Purl on front, knit on back — 0 Yarn over — \ skp — / k2tog

SHAWL BODY

Continue to work the first stitch of every row as k1 tbl, yo, and the last stitch of every row as sl 1 wyif.

Rows 1–12: Work rows 1–12 of Center Triangle Stockinette.

Rows 13–24: Work Right-Leaning Stockinette, Center Triangle Reverse Stockinette, and Left-Leaning Stockinette.

Rows 25–36: Work Right-Leaning Stockinette, Right-Leaning Reverse Stockinette, Center Triangle Stockinette, Left-Leaning Reverse Stockinette, Left-Leaning Stockinette

Rows 37–48: Work Right-Leaning Stockinette, Right-Leaning Reverse Stockinette, Right-Leaning Stockinette, Center Triangle Reverse Stockinette, Left-Leaning Stockinette, Left-Leaning Reverse Stockinette, Left-Leaning Stockinette.

Continue in this manner until there are 8 groups of Right-Leaning Stockinette followed by Right-Leaning Reverse Stockinette patterns, and 8 groups of Left-Leaning Reverse Stockinette followed by Left-Leaning Stockinette on each side of the center triangle. Cut the yarn. Weave in ends.

This project was knit with: Artyarns Cameo, 75% cashmere/25% mohair, 3½ oz/100g =370yd/338m per skein, 2 skeins color #130. To find equivalent yarn brands from other makers, see the Yarn Substitution Chart on page 142.

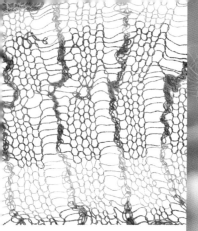

La Parisienne Collar

Skill Level

● ● ● ●

Easy

TECHNIQUE

Alternating Center
Double Decrease Pattern
(page 60)

Finished Measurements

24"/61cm circumference x 8"/20cm depth

Materials

Yarn: 250yd/229m of **(0)** lace weight yarn, kid mohair and silk blend

• Color A: 50yd/46m, in rust

• Color B: 50yd/46m, in charcoal

• Color C: 50yd/46m, in navy

• Color D: 50yd/46m, in beige

• Color E: 50yd/46m, in brown

Knitting needles: 4 mm (size 6 U.S.) 40"/100cm circular, *or size to obtain gauge.*

Stitch marker

Yarn needle

Gauge

20 stitches and 24 rows = 4"/10cm in Lace Pattern Stitch

Always take time to check your gauge.

Special Stitch

Lace Pattern:

Round 1: *Yo, sl 2tog, k1, p2sso, yo, k3; repeat from *.

Repeat Round 1 for pattern.

Instructions

Using Möbius cast-on (see page 18), cast on 111 sts with A.

Note: With this cast-on you have a total of 222 sts on the needle. Place a marker to identify the start of the round.

Rounds 1–2: With A, work Lace Pattern Stitch.

Rounds 3–5: With B, work Lace Pattern Stitch.

Rounds 6–9: With C, work Lace Pattern Stitch.

Rounds 10–17: With D, work Lace Pattern Stitch.

Rounds 18–23: With E, work Lace Pattern Stitch.

Round 24: Remove marker and bind off in Lace Pattern Stitch as follows: *Yo, bind off, sl 2tog, k1, p2sso, bind off, yo, bind off, k1, bind off, k1, bind off, k1, bind off; repeat from * until there is 1 stitch remaining. Cut yarn. Pull yarn through remaining st. Weave in ends.

This project was knit with:

Artyarns Silk Mohair, 60% mohair/40% silk 0.9oz/25g = 312 yd/285m per skein, one skein each in color #s 263, 264, 252, 249, and 248. To find equivalent yarn brands from other makers, see the Yarn Substitution Chart on page 142.

Cable

CABLES ARE VERY MUCH LIKE RAILROAD CROSSINGS. IN KNITTED FABRIC THEY ARE FORMED BY KNITTING STITCHES OUT OF TURN, RESULTING IN A DESIGN THAT IS TWISTED. BECAUSE THEY TEND TO PINCH THE FABRIC AND DISTORT IT SOMEWHAT, IT IS USUALLY NECESSARY TO KEEP THE FABRIC FROM PUCKERING BY KNITTING SEVERAL ROWS WITHOUT CROSSING BEFORE CROSSING THE STITCHES AGAIN. A GENERAL RULE OF THUMB IS THAT THE MORE STITCHES BEING CROSSED OR KNIT OUT OF ORDER, THE MORE ROWS BETWEEN SUBSEQUENT CROSSINGS. THE STITCHES CROSSED ARE EITHER POSITIONED BEHIND OR IN FRONT OF THE STITCHES THEY ARE CROSSING.

PROJECTS IN THIS CHAPTER

Gossamer Collar
Courtyard Drape (right)
Tiger's Paw Scarf (left)
Artful Dodger Scarf

CABLE TECHNIQUES

Here you will see how to match a cable on two sides, so the reverse has a similar pattern, and also how to create a different pattern from one side to the other. The instructions are written to use one or two cable needles to hold the stitches that are being crossed and knitted out of turn. An extra set of short (5¼"/13cm) double-pointed needles can be used instead. Once again, as shown in previous chapters, a rib stitch will help hide crossings on the reverse and create the appearance of two separately and deliberately designed sides.

ABBREVIATION

C6F: Sl 6 sts to cable needle and hold in front of work, [k1, p1] 3 times, [k1, p1] from cn 3 times.

Cast on 24 stitches.

Rows 1–3: [K1, p1] 9 times, [p1, k1] 3 times.

Row 4: [K1, p1] 3 times, C6F, [p1, k1] 3 times.

Repeat Rows 1–4 for pattern.

Simple cable patterns, defined as one group of stitches crossing over a second group on a row, can be modified so that they are similar on both sides by knitting them in rib pattern. Convert the cable pattern you wish to follow to a matched 1x1 or 2x2 rib. It is important that you cross the stitches so the entire grouping (1 knit and 1 purl in 1x1 rib, or 2 knits and 2 purls in 2x2 rib) is lifted. For example, you can see here in the 1x1 rib example that 3 groups of stitches (6 total) are crossed over 3 groups (6 total) of stitches. Panels used to offset the cables and make them more prominent also need to be knitted in patterns that are similar on both sides. In this example, the Seed stitch is used. ■

ABBREVIATIONS

C2/2/2F: Sl 2 to cn1 and hold in front of work, sl 2 to cn2 and hold in back of work, k2 from left needle, p2 from cn2, k2 from cn1.

C2/2/2B: Wyif, sl 2 to cn1 and hold in back of work, sl 2 to cn2 and hold behind cn1, k2 from left needle, sl 2 from cn1 to left needle, sl 2 from cn2 to left needle, p2, k2.

C2F: Sl 1 to cn and hold in front of work, k1, k1 from cn.

C2B: Sl 1 st to cn and hold in back of work, k1, k1 from cn.

Cast on 48 stitches.

Row 1: K1, *k2, p2; repeat from * to last 3 sts, k3.

Rows 2, 6, 10, 14, and 18: K1, p2, k2, p2, C2/2/2B, p2, k2, p2, C2F, p2, k2, p2, C2B, p2, k2, p2, C2/2/2F, p2, k2, p2, k1.

Rows 4, 8, 12, 16, and 20: K1, [p2, k2] 4 times, p2, C2F, p2, k2, p2, C2B, [p2, k2] 4 times, p2, k1.

Row 5: K3, p2, C2/2/2F, p2, [k2, p2] twice, C2/2/2B, p2, [k2, p2] twice, C2/2/2B, p2, k3.

Row 7: K3, p2, k2, p2, C2/2/2F, p2, k2, p2, C2/2/2B, p2, k2, p2, C2/2/2B, p2, k2, p2, k3.

Row 9: K1, [k2, p2] 3 times, C2/2/2F, p2, C2/2/2B, p2, C2/2/2B, p2, [k2, p2] 3 times, k3.

Row 11: K1, [k2, p2] 5 times, C2/2/2F, p2, [k2, p2] 4 times, k3.

Row 13: K1, [k2, p2] 4 times, C2/2/2B, p2, C2/2/2F, p2, [k2, p2] 3 times, k3.

Row 15: K1, [k2, p2] 3 times, C2/2/2B, p2, C2/2/2B, p2, C2/2/2F, p2, [k2, p2] twice, k3.

Row 17: K1, [k2, p2] twice, C2/2/2B, p2, k2, p2, C2/2/2B, p2, k2, p2, C2/2/2/F, p2, k2, p2, k3.

Row 19: K3, p2, C2/2/2B, [p2, k2] twice, p2, C2/2/2B, [p2, k2] twice, p2, C2/2/2F, p2, k3.

Row 21: K1, C2/2/2B, [p2, k2] 3 times, p2, C2/2/2B, [p2, k2] 3 times, p2, C2/2/2F, k1.

It is entirely possible to cross knit stitches on both sides of the work to create two different cable patterns, one on each side, using the rib pattern. In this example, where 2x2 rib is used, the two sets of knit stitches have been crossed in front of the set of purl stitches to maintain the k2, p2 sequence. Therefore, the cable patterns on one side's knit stitches will be hidden in the purl stitches on the other side. ■

Row 9: With A, k4, *k2, p1, C2/1/2B, k3; repeat from * to last st, k1.

Row 13: With A, k4, *C2/1/2B, p1, k5; repeat from * to last st, k1.

Repeat rows 1–16 for pattern.

Stripes on one side, and traveling cables on the other, are created by slipping the cabled stitches every time yarn B is worked. Stitches are slipped with the yarn in front on the striped side, and with the yarn in back on the cable side. Notice that the garter pattern panel in the two colors between every cable emphasizes the cable.

As you work through these exercises, think about how to convert traditional cable patterns to be reversible. As seen here, the cables are worked in various combinations of rib patterns, and a background pattern is needed to emphasize the cable. It is important to decide whether the cable will be similar on the reverse, which requires the full group of stitches to be crossed, or whether the cable will appear only on one side, which requires the crossings that leave the purl stitches intact. Make sure to choose an appropriate background pattern that emphasizes rather than interferes with the cable. Soft yarns or larger needles will keep the cables from becoming overly stiff. ∎

ABBREVIATIONS

C2/1/2F: Sl 2 to cn1 and hold in front of work, sl 1 to cn2 and hold in back of work, k2 from left needle, p1 from cn2, k2 from cn1.

C2/1/2B: Wyif, sl 2 to cn1 and hold in back of work, sl 1 to cn2 and hold behind cn1, k2 from left needle, sl 2 from cn1 to left needle, sl 1 from cn2 to left needle, p1, k2.

With A, cast on 38 stitches.

Row 1: With A, k4, *C2/1/2F, p1, k5; repeat from * to last st, k1.

Rows 2, 6, 10, and 14: With A, k4, [p2, k1] twice, p2, k3, [p2, k1] twice, p2, k3, [p2, k1] twice, p2, k4.

Rows 3, 7, 11, and 15: With B, k4, *[sl 2b, p1] twice, sl 2b, k3; repeat from * to last st, k1.

Rows 4, 8, 12, and 16: With B, k4, *[sl 2f, k1] twice, sl 2f, k3; repeat from * to last st, k1.

Row 5: With A, k4, *k2, p1, C2/1/2F, k3; repeat from * to last st, k1.

ABBREVIATIONS

C2/2/2F: Sl 2 to cn1 and hold in front of work, sl 2 to cn2 and hold in back of work, k2 from left needle, p2 from cn2, k2 from cn1.

C2/2/2B: Wyif, sl 2 to cn1 and hold in back of work, sl 2 to cn2 and hold behind cn1, k2 from left needle, sl 2 from cn1 to left needle, sl 2 from cn2 to left needle, p2, k2.

Cast on 24 stitches.

Rows 1, 5, and 9: K1, [k2, p2] 5 times, k3.

Row 2 and all even rows: K1, [p2, k2] 5 times, p2, k1.

Row 3: K1, [k2, p2] twice, C2/2/2B, [p2, k2] twice, k1.

Row 7: K1, k2, p2, C2/2/2B, p2, C2/2/2F, p2, k2, k1.

Row 11: K1, C2/2/2B, [p2, k2] twice, p2, C2/2/2F, k1.

Repeat rows 1–12 for pattern.

This cable is hidden in the purl part of the rib on the back. Instead of crossing the entire group of stitches as in the previous exercise, you cross only the knit stitches, leaving the purl stitches intact on the back of the work. This will hide all the cable crossings on the opposite side, giving the appearance that it is designed in a simple rib stitch pattern. ■

Gossamer Collar

Skill Level
• • • •
Beginner

TECHNIQUE
*Cable Pattern Similar
on Both Sides (page 70)*

WHISPER CLOUD LIGHT

Finished Measurements

Approximately 6"/15cm x wide 40"/102cm long

Materials

Yarn: 624yd/570m total of **1** super fine yarn, mohair and silk blend

• Color A: 312yd/285m, in variegated cream and melon

• Color B: 312yd/285m, in variegated cream and peach

Knitting needles: 5 mm (size 8 U.S.) *or size to obtain gauge*

Cable needle (cn)

Yarn needle

Gauge

34 stitches and 24 rows = 4"/10cm in pattern stitch

Always take time to check your gauge.

Abbreviations

C6F: Place 6 sts on cable needle and bring to front, [k1, p1] 3 times into 6 sts on left needle, then [k1, p1] 3 times into 6 sts on cn; turn; [k1, p1] 6 times, turn; [k1, p1] 6 times across same 12 sts.

C6B: Place 6 sts on cn and bring to back, [k1, p1] 3 times into 6 sts on left needle, then [k1, p1] 3 times into 6 sts on cn; turn, [k1, p1] 6 times, turn; [k1, p1] 6 times across same 12 sts.

Instructions

Note: This scarf is knitted in two parts. The first half is the left-leaning half, skewing left, and the second half is the right-leaning half, skewing right. Colors A and B are worked individually, two rows of color A followed by four rows of color B. Carry yarns up from behind, twisting yarn not being used around yarn that will be used next.

FIRST HALF

With A, cast on 60 stitches.

Row 1: With A, [(k1, p1) 3 times, turn] twice, [k1, p1] 3 times, C6F 4 times, [(k1, p1) 3 times, turn] twice, [k1, p1] 3 times.

Row 2: With A, *k1 p1; repeat from * to end of row.

Rows 3–6: With B, *k1, p1; repeat from * to end of row.

Row 7: With A, C6F 5 times.

Row 8: Repeat row 2.

Rows 9–12: Repeat rows 3–6.

Repeat rows 1–12 until scarf measures 20"/51cm.

SECOND HALF

Row 1: With A, [(k1, p1) 3 times, turn] twice, [k1, p1] 3 times, C6B 4 times, [(k1, p1) 3 times, turn] twice, [k1, p1] 3 times.

Row 2: With A, *k1 p1; repeat from * to end of row.

Rows 3–6: With B, *k1, p1; repeat from * to end of row.

Row 7: With A, C6B 5 times.

Row 8: Repeat row 2.

Rows 9–12: Repeat rows 3–6.

Repeat rows 1–12 until scarf measures 40"/102cm.

Bind off all sts. Cut yarn, weave in ends.

This project was knit with:
Artyarns Silk Mohair, 60% mohair, 40% silk, 0.9oz/25g = 312 yd/285m per skein, one skein each of color #413 and color #405. To find equivalent yarn brands from other makers, see the Yarn Substitution Chart on page 142.

Courtyard Drape

Skill Level
● ● ● ●
Easy

TECHNIQUE
Two-Color Cable Pattern
(page 72)
and Cable Pattern on One Side,
Rib Pattern on Reverse
(page 73)

FREESTYLE WRAPPING

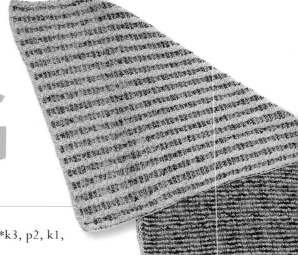

Finished Measurements

25"/64cm wide x 42"/107cm long

Materials

Yarn A: 800yd/732m of  4 medium weight yarn, 100% cashmere, in camel

Yarn B: 800yd/732m of 4 medium weight yarn, 100% merino wool, in variegated blue, rust, brown

Knitting needles: 5 mm (size 8 U.S.) *or size to obtain gauge*

2 cable needles

Gauge

24 stitches and 30 rows = 4"/10cm in pattern stitch

Always take time to check your gauge.

Abbreviation

C2/1/2F: Sl 2 to cn1 and hold in front of work, sl 1 to cn2 and hold in back of work, k2 from left needle, p1 from back cn, k2 from front cn.

Pattern

Cable Pattern Stitch:

Row 1: With A, k1, (k2, p1, k2), *p3, (k2, p1, k2); repeat from * to last st, k1.

Row 2: With A, k1, (p2, k1, p2), *k3, p2, k1, p2; repeat from * to last st, k1.

Row 3: With B, k1, (sl 2b, p1, sl 2b), *p3, (sl 2b, p1, sl 2b); repeat from * to last st, k1.

Row 4: With B, k1, (sl 2f, k1, sl 2f), *k3, (sl 2f, k1, sl 2f); repeat from * to last st, k1.

Row 5: With A, k1, C2/1/2F, *p3, C2/1/2F; repeat from * to last st, k1.

Row 6: With A, repeat row 2.

Rows 7–8: With B, repeat rows 3–4.

Rows 9–12: Repeat rows 5–8.

Instructions

With A, CO 159 sts.

Work rows 1–12 of Cable Pattern Stitch until blanket measures 42"/107cm. Bind off sts, weave in ends.

This project was knit with:

Artyarns Cashmere 5, 100% cashmere, 1¾oz/50g = 102yd/93m per skein, 8 skeins color #270; Artyarns Supermerino, 100% merino wool, 1¾oz/50g = 104yd/95m per skein, 8 skeins color #173. To find equivalent yarn brands from other makers, see the Yarn Substitution Chart on page 142.

Tiger's Paw Scarf

Skill Level
• • • •
Intermediate

TECHNIQUE

*Cable Pattern on One Side,
Rib Pattern on Reverse
(page 73)*

NATURAL BEAUTY

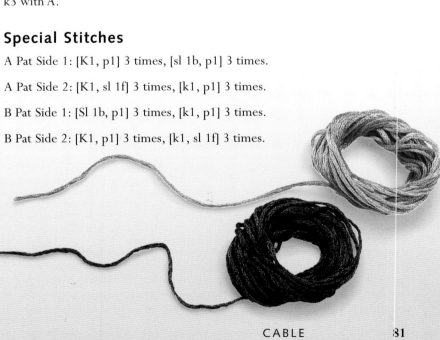

Finished Measurements

3½"/9cm wide x 24"/61cm long

Materials

Yarn: 340yd/310m of 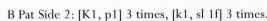 light weight yarn, silk

- Color A: 170yd/155m in variegated black, brown, red
- Color B: 170yd/155m in salmon

Knitting needles: 3.75 mm (size 5 U.S.) 16"/40cm circular, *or size to obtain gauge*

Stitch marker

2 cable needles

Stitch holder

Extra needle for 3-needle bind-off

Gauge

24 sts and 22 rows = 4"/10cm in pattern stitch

Always take time to check your gauge.

Abbreviations

C3/3/3F: Sl 3 sts to cn1 and hold in front of work, sl 3 sts to cn2 and hold in back of work, k3 from left needle with B, k3 with A from cn2, k3 with B from cn1.

C3/3/3B: Sl 3 sts to cn1 and hold in back of work, sl 3 sts to cn2 and hold in back of cn1, k3 from left needle with A, sl 3 sts from cn1 back to left needle, sl 3 sts from cn2 back to left needle, k3 with A k3 with A.

Special Stitches

A Pat Side 1: [K1, p1] 3 times, [sl 1b, p1] 3 times.

A Pat Side 2: [K1, sl 1f] 3 times, [k1, p1] 3 times.

B Pat Side 1: [Sl 1b, p1] 3 times, [k1, p1] 3 times.

B Pat Side 2: [K1, p1] 3 times, [k1, sl 1f] 3 times.

Instructions

Using the provisional cast-on (page 17), with A, CO 78 sts onto circular needles. Join stitches to work in the round. Place marker to identify start of round, slipping it throughout.

Round 1: *K3 with A, k3 with B; repeat from * to end of round, carrying the yarn not in use loosely behind.

Round 2: [K3 with A, C3/3/3F] 3 times, *k3 with A, k3 with B; repeat from* to end of round.

Rounds 3–5: Repeat round 1.

Round 6: K3 with A, k3 with B, [C3/3/3B, k3 with B] 3 times, *k3 with A, k3 with B; repeat from * to end of round.

Rounds 7–11: Work rounds 1–11 one more time, and then work rounds 2–5.

Repeat round 1 until piece measures 22"/56cm, ending last round 2 sts before marker, inc1, inc1. Next round: [K3 with A, k3 with B] 6 times, k3 with A, k1 with B. Place 40 sts just knitted onto stitch holder.

Rows 1–2: With A, k1, *k1, p1; repeat from* to last st, k1.

Rows 3–4: With B, k1, *k1, p1; repeat from * to last st, k1.

Row 5: With B, k1, *[k1, p1] 3 times, [sl 1b, p1] 3 times; repeat from * to last 3 sts, k1, p1, k1.

Row 6: With B, k2, p1, *[k1, sl 1f] 3 times, [k1, p1] 3 times; repeat from * to last st, k1.

Row 7: With A, k1, *[sl 1b, p1] 3 times, [k1, p1] 3 times; repeat from * to last 3 sts, sl 1b, p1, k1.

Row 8: With A, k2, sl 1f, *[k1, p1] 3 times, [k1, sl 1f] 3 times; repeat from * to last st, k1.

Rows 9–20: Repeat rows 5–8 three more times.

CONTINUE WITH ONE-ROW STRIPE SEQUENCE

Rows 1–2: With B, k1, *k1, p1; repeat from * to last st, k1.

Row 3: With A, k1, *k1, p1; repeat from * to last st, k1. Slide sts to other end of needle.

Row 4: With B, k1, *k1, p1; repeat from * to last st, k1. Slide sts to other end of needle.

Row 5: Repeat row 3.

Row 6: Repeat row 4.

Rows 7–8: Repeat rows 3–4.

BEGIN DIAGONAL STRIPE PATTERN

Row 1: With A, k1, repeat A Pat Side 1 to last 3 sts, k1, p1, k1.

Row 2: With A, k2, p1, repeat A Pat Side 2 to last st, k1.

Row 3: With B, k2, p1, repeat B Pat Side 1 to last st, k1.

Row 4: With B, k1, repeat B Pat Side 2 to last 3 sts, k1, p1, k1.

Row 5: With A, k1, sl 1b, p1, repeat A Pat Side 1 to last st, k1

Row 6: With A, k1, repeat A Pat Side 2 to last 3 sts, k1, sl 1f, k1.

Row 7: With B, k2, p1, k1, p1, repeat B Pat Side 1 to last 5 sts, [k1, p1] twice, k1.

Row 8: With B, k1, [k1, p1] twice, [k1, sl 1f] 3 times, repeat B Pat Side 2 to last 5 sts, [k1, p1] twice, k1.

Row 9: With A, k1, [sl 1b, p1] twice, repeat A Pat Side 1 to last 11 sts, [k1, p1] 3 times, [sl 1b, p1] twice, k1.

Row 10: With A, k1, [k1, sl 1f] twice, [k1, p1] 3 times, repeat A Pat Side 2 to last 5 sts, [k1, sl 1f] twice, k1.

Row 11: With B, k1, [k1, p1] 3 times, repeat B Pat Side 1 to last 9 sts, [sl 1b, p1] 3 times, k1, p1, k1.

Row 12: With B, k2, p1, [k1, sl 1f] 3 times, repeat B Pat Side 2 to last 7 sts, [k1, p1] 3 times, k1.

Row 13: With A, k1, [sl 1b, p1] 3 times, repeat A Pat Side 1 to last 9 st, [k1, p1] 3 times, sl 1b, p1, k1.

Row 14: With A, k2, sl 1f, [k1, p1] 3 times, repeat A Pat Side 2 to last st, k1.

Row 15: With B, k1, sl 1b, p1, [k1, p1] 3 times, repeat B Pat Side 1 to last 7 sts, [sl 1b, p1] 3 times, k1.

Row 16: With B, k1, [k1, sl 1f] 3 times, repeat B Pat Side 2 to last 9 sts, [k1, p1] 3 times, k1, sl 1f, k1.

Row 17: With A, k2, p1, [sl 1b, p1] 3 times, repeat A Pat Side 1 to last 7 sts, [k1, p1] 3 times, k1.

Row 18: With A, k1, [k1, p1] 3 times, repeat A Pat Side 2 to last 9 sts, [k1, sl 1f] 3 times, k1, p1, k1.

Row 19: With B, k1, [sl 1b, p1] twice, [k1, p1] 3 times, repeat B Pat Side 1 to last 5 sts, [sl 1b, p1] twice, k1.

Row 20: With B, k1, [k1, sl 1f] twice, repeat B Pat Side 2 to last 11 st, [k1, p1] 3 times, [k1, sl 1f] twice, k1.

Work rows 3–8 of One-Row Stripe Sequence. With outsides together, use the 3-needle bind-off (see page 19) to join to 40 held sts and form a loop. Remove waste yarn from the provisional cast-on, and separate the stitches onto 2 needles equally, so that 40 stitches on the cabled side are on one needle, and 41 sts on the opposite side are on the second needle. Using A and the 3-needle bind-off, attach the two sides together.

Cut yarn, weave in ends.

This project was knit with:
Artyarns Silk Pearl, 100% silk, 13¼ oz/50g = 170yd/155m per skein, 1 skein in color #166, 1 skein in color #2222. To find equivalent yarn brands from other makers, see the Yarn Substitution Chart on page 142.

Artful Dodger Scarf

Skill Level
● ● ● ●
Intermediate

TECHNIQUE
*Cable Pattern Different
on Each Side (page 71)*

STEAL THIS SCARF

Finished Measurements

5"/13cm wide x 46"/117cm long

Materials

Yarn: 288yd/263m of  light weight yarn, wool, in beige

Knitting needles: 3.5 mm (size 6 U.S.) *or size to obtain gauge*

2 cable needles

Gauge

22 stitches and 24 rows = 4"/10cm in Stockinette stitch

Always take time to check your gauge.

Abbreviations

C2/2/2F: Sl 2 sts to cn1 and hold in front of work, sl 2 sts to cn2 and hold in back of work, k2 from left needle, p2 from cn2, k2 from cn1.

C2/2/2B: Sl 2 sts to cn1 and hold in back of work, sl 2 sts to cn2 and hold behind cn1, k2 from left needle, sl 2 sts from cn1 to left needle, sl 2 sts from cn2 to left needle, p2, k2.

C2F: Sl 1 st to cn and hold in front, k1, k1 from cn.

C2B: Sl 1 st to cn and hold in back, k1, k1 from cn.

Instructions

CO 48 sts.

UPSIDE-DOWN V DESIGN

Row 1: K1, [k2, p2] 11 times, k3.

Row 2: K1, p2, k2, p2, C2/2/2B, p2, k2, p2, C2F, p2, k2, p2, C2B, p2, k2, p2, C2/2/2B, p2, k2, p2, k1

Row 3: K1, C2/2/2F, p2, [k2, p2] 3 times, C2/2/2F, p2, [k2, p2] 3 times, C2/2/2B, k1.

Row 4: K1, p2, [k2, p2] 4 times, C2F, p2, k2, p2, C2B, p2, [k2, p2] 4 times, k1.

Row 5: Repeat Row 1.

Row 6: Repeat Row 2.

Row 7: K3, p2, C2/2/2F, p2, [k2, p2] twice, C2/2/2F, p2, [k2, p2] twice, C2/2/2B, p2, k3.

Row 8: Repeat Row 4.

Row 9: Repeat Row 1.

Row 10: Repeat Row 2.

Row 11: K3, p2, k2, p2 C2/2/2F, p2, k2, p2, C2/2/2F, p2, k2, p2, C2/2/2B, p2, k2, p2, k3.

Row 12: Repeat Row 4.

Row 13: Repeat Row 1.

Row 14: Repeat Row 2.

Row 15: K3, p2, [k2, p2] twice, C2/2/2F, p2, C2/2/2F, p2, C2/2/2B, p2, [k2, p2] twice, k3.

Row 16: Repeat Row 4.

Row 17: Repeat Row 1.

Row 18: Repeat Row 2.

Row 19: K3, p2, [k2, p2] 3 times, C2/2/2F, p2, C2/2/2B, p2, [k2, p2] 3 times, k3.

Row 20: Repeat Row 4.

Row 21: Repeat Row 1.

Row 22: Repeat Row 2.

Row 23: K3, p2, [k2, p2] 4 times, C2/2/2F, p2, [k2, p2] 4 times, k3.

Row 24: Repeat row 4.

Repeat rows 1–24 four more times (five times total).

DIAMOND SHAPE

Row 1: K1, [k2, p2] 11 times, k3.

Row 2: K1, p2, k2, p2, C2/2/2B, p2, k2, p2, C2F, p2, k2, p2, C2B, p2, k2, p2, C2/2/2B, p2, k2, p2, k1.

Row 3: K3, p2, [k2, p2] 3 times, C2/2/2B, p2, C2/2/2F, p2, [k2, p2] 3 times, k3.

Row 4: K1, p2, [k2, p2] 4 times, C2F, p2, k2, p2, C2B, p2, [k2, p2] 4 times, k1.

Row 5: Repeat Row 1.

Row 6: Repeat Row 2.

Row 7: K3, p2, [k2, p2] twice, C2/2/2B, p2, C2/2/2BF, p2, C2/2/2F, p2, [k2, p2] twice, k3.

Row 8: Repeat row 4.

Row 9: Repeat row 1.

Row 10: Repeat row 2.

Row 11: K3, p2, k2, p2 C2/2/2B, p2, k2, p2, C2/2/2F, p2, k2,p2, C2/2/2F, p2, k2, p2, k3.

Row 12: Repeat row 4.

Row 13: Repeat row 1.

Row 14: Repeat row 2.

Row 15: K3, p2, C2/2/2B, p2, [k2, p2] twice, C2/2/2F, p2, [k2, p2] twice, C2/2/2F, p2, k3.

Row 16: Repeat row 4.

Row 17: Repeat row 1.

Row 18: Repeat row 2.

Row 19: K1, C2/2/2B, p2, [k2, p2] 3 times, C2/2/2F, p2, [k2, p2] 3 times, C2/2/2F, k1.

Row 20: Repeat row 4.

Rows 21–44: Repeat rows 1–24 of Upside-Down V Design.

V SHAPE

Repeat rows 1–20 of Diamond Shape and then repeat [rows 21-24 of Upside Down V Design followed by rows 1-20 of Diamond Shape] four times. Bind off all stitches.

Cut yarn, weave in ends.

This project was knit with:
Artyarns Ultramerino 6, 100% merino wool, 3½ oz/100g = 274yd/250m per skein, 1 skein color #257. To find equivalent yarn brands from other makers, see the Yarn Substitution Chart on page 142.

Double Knitting

PROBABLY THE MOST FLEXIBLE TECHNIQUE FOR PRODUCING REVERSIBLE DESIGNS THAT INCORPORATE MANY COLORS IS DOUBLE KNITTING. ALL THE COLOR CHANGES AND TAILS ARE HIDDEN BETWEEN TWO LAYERS OF FABRIC, AND YOU CAN HAVE A NICE SMOOTH STOCKINETTE STITCH FACE ON BOTH SIDES.

IT TAKES MORE TIME TO KNIT A DOUBLE-KNITTED PIECE THAN A REGULAR KNITTED PIECE, BUT THE ADVANTAGES OF DOUBLE-WARM FABRIC AND EASY GOOD LOOKS MAKE THE EXTRA TIME WORTHWHILE.

PROJECTS IN THIS CHAPTER

Bauhaus Lights Scarf
SoHo Hat
Bowery Trio (in photo)
Ribbon Candy Scarf
Charcoal Möbius Collar
Southport Shawl

DOUBLE KNITTING TECHNIQUES

There are two methods to create a double layer of knitted fabric, that is, two layers that are created at the same time: two-stranded double knitting and slip stitch knitting with one strand at a time. In two-stranded double knitting, the two yarns are carried together at the same time (see page 20 for how they are worked), and every row is worked once. In slip stitch knitting, only one strand is used at a time and every row is worked twice.

A common technique in both methods is to use rib patterns to present both sides of the work as though they were knitted in Stockinette stitch. The weaving (slipping with yarn in front or in back) is hidden, and all you see are the knit stitches in the 1x1 rib pattern used throughout this chapter. As you work two rows of each color, make sure to twist the previous color with the working color to create a nice edge (see page 21).

Two-Strand Method, Different Sides

The two-strand method can be used to make designs that are different on each side. Rather than always knitting one stitch with one color and purling the next stitch with the second color, here you'll sometimes knit a stitch with color A and purl the companion stitch with color A as well.

With A, cast on 26 sts.

Row 1: K2A, p1B, [k1B, p1B, (k1A, p1B) 3 times] twice, k1B, p1B, [k1A, p1B] twice, k1A.

Row 2 and all even rows: Work remaining stitches as they appear (same color, same stitch).

Row 3: K1A, [k1A, p1B, (k1B, p1B) 3 times] 3 times, k1A.

Row 5: K1A, [(k1B, p1B) 3 times, k1A, p1B] 3 times, k1A.

Row 7: K1A, [k1A, p1B] twice, [k1B, p1B, (k1A, p1B) 3 times] twice, k1B, p1B, k1A, p1B, k1A.

Row 9: K2A, p1A, [k1B, p1A, (k1A, p1A) 3 times] twice, k1B, p1A, [k1A, p1A] twice, k1A.

Row 11: K1A, [k1A, p1A, (k1B, p1A) 3 times] 3 times, k1A.

Row 13: K1A, [(k1B, p1A) 3 times, k1A, p1A] 3 times, k1A.

Row 15: K1A, [k1A, p1A] twice, [k1B, p1A, (k1A, p1A) 3 times] twice, k1B, p1A, k1A, p1A, k1A.

Bind off as follows: With A, k1, [k1, bind off, p1, bind off] 9 times, k1, bind off. ∎

In this example, you knit a piece that has a similar pattern on both sides but has opposite colors on each side.

Note: In two-stranded knitting, always carry the two strands together. When knitting, make sure both are in back of the work. When purling, make sure both strands are in front of the work (see page 21).

With A, cast on 28 sts. Attach B.

Setup Row: K1A, [k1A, p1B] to last st, k1A.

Row 1: K1B, [k1B, p1A] 6 times, k1A, p1B, [k1B p1A] 6 times, k1B.

Row 2: K1A, [k1A, p1B] 5 times, k1B, p1A, k1A, p1B, k1B, p1A, [k1A, p1B] 5 times, k1A.

Row 3: K1B, [k1B, p1A] 4 times, [k1A, p1B, k1B, p1A] twice, k1A, p1B, [k1B, p1A] 4 times, k1B.

Row 4: K1A, [k1A, p1B] 3 times, [k1B, p1A, k1A, p1B] 3 times, k1B, p1A, [k1A, p1B] 3 times, k1A.

Row 5: K1B, [k1B, p1A] twice, [k1A, p1B, k1B, p1A] 4 times, k1A, p1B, [k1B, p1A] twice, k1B.

Row 6: K1A, k1A, p1B, [k1B, p1A, k1A, p1B] 5 times, k1B, p1A, k1A, p1B, k1A.

Row 7: Repeat row 5.

Row 8: Repeat row 4.

Row 9: Repeat row 3.

Row 10: Repeat row 2.

Row 11: Repeat row 1.

Row 12: K1A, [k1A, p1B] to last st, k1A.

Bind off as follows: with A, k1, [k1, bind off, p1, bind off] 9 times, k1, bind off.

When planning a design such as this one, where there is not much repetition but the pattern is similar on the two sides, graph your design, and follow the chart

☒ **Color A**	☐ **Color B**

by knitting with the yarn that you wish to present on the side facing you, and then purling with the yarn that you wish to present on the opposite side, which in this pattern is the second color.

This type of design is much more easily worked in two-stranded knitting than with the slip stitch method, since you can change colors A and B simultaneously. Instead of having to keep track of the color changes in the pattern twice per row, you only need to keep track once per row. ∎

Slip Stitch Method, Different Sides

This example shows how to use the slip stitch method to produce a design that is completely different on each side.

When working with color A, you'll slip some stitches and knit other stitches. Then you'll work the same row with color B, this time slipping the stitches that were previously knitted in color A and knitting the stitches that were previously slipped. In order to knit this way, you slide the stitches from one end of a circular or double-pointed needle to the other so that the new color is accessible to be picked up and used.

This method is ideal for patterns where there is a great deal of repetition but the two sides are different.

With A, cast on 22 sts.

Row 1: With B, k1, *p1, sl 1b, p1, k1; repeat from * to last st, k1, slide.

Row 2: With A, k1, *sl 1f, k1, sl 1f, sl 1b; repeat from * to last st, k1, turn.

Row 3: With B, k1, *p1, k1, sl 1f, k1; repeat from * to last st, k1, slide.

Row 4: With A, k1, *sl 1f, k1, p1, k1; repeat from * to last st, k1, turn.

Row 5: With B, k1, *sl 1f, sl 1b, sl 1f, k1; repeat from * to last st, k1, slide.

Row 6: With A, k1, *p1, k1, p1, sl 1b; repeat from * to last st, k1, turn.

Row 7: Repeat row 3.

Row 8: With A, k1, *sl 1f, sl 1b, p1, sl 1b; repeat from * to last st, k1, turn.

Row 9: Repeat row 1.

Row 10: Repeat row 6.

Row 11: With B, k1, *p1, sl 1b, sl 1f, sl 1b; repeat from * to last st, k1, slide.

Row 12: Repeat row 4.

Repeat rows 1–12 for pattern. ■

You can find instructions for making this alternate version of the SoHo Hat (page 97) on our website at www.larkcrafts.com/bonus.

Bauhaus Lights Scarf

Skill Level
• • • •
Easy

TECHNIQUE
*Slip Stitch Method,
Different Sides
(page 92)*

94

Finished Measurements

4¾"/12cm wide x 50"/127cm long

Materials

Yarn: 300 yd/274m of (4) medium weight yarn, cashmere

• Color A: 150yd/137m in navy

• Color B: 150yd/137m in pale blue

Knitting needles: 4.5 mm (size 7 U.S.) 16"/40cm or 24"/60cm circular *or size to obtain gauge*

Gauge

16 stitches and 24 rows = 4"/10cm

Always take time to check your gauge.

Patterns

TWEED AND SOLID PATTERN

Multiple of 8 sts plus 7.

Row 1 (Tweed side): With A, sl 1f, *k1, sl 1f; repeat from * across row, turn—A and B yarns on same side.

Row 2 (Solid side): If first time, attach B, otherwise carry it up side, twisting over A. With B, k1, *sl 1f, k1; repeat from * to end of row, turn—A yarn on other end.

Row 3 (Tweed side): With B, *p1, [k1, p1] 3 times, sl 1b; repeat from * to last 7 sts, p1, [k1, p1] 3 times—A and B on same side.

Row 4 (Solid side): Carry A up side, twisting over B. With A, sl 1b, *p1, sl 1b; repeat from * to end of row—B on other end. Slide sts to other end of needle.

Row 5 (Solid side): With B, k1, *sl 1f, k1; repeat from * to end of row, turn—A and B on same side.

Row 6 (Tweed side): Carry B up side, twisting over A. With B, *p1, (k1, p1) 3 times, sl 1b; rep from * to last 5 sts, p1, (k1, p1) twice—A on other end. Slide sts to other end of needle.

Bauhaus Lights Scarf

10-ROW STRIPED PATTERN

Worked in [k1, p1] rib throughout. When working the Tweed side, *p1, k1; repeat from * to last st, p1. When working the Solid side, *k1, p1; repeat from * to last st, k1.

Variation 1: Alternate 2 rows B, 2 rows A, 1 row B (slide), 2 rows A (slide), 1 row B, 2 rows A.

Variation 2: Alternate 3 rows B (slide), 1 row A, 2 rows B, 1 row A (slide), 1 row B, 2 rows A.

Variation 3: Alternate 1 row B (slide), 2 rows A (slide), 1 row B, 1 row A (slide), 1 row B, 1 row A (slide), 3 rows B.

Variation 4: Alternate 2 rows B, 2 rows A, 2 rows B, 1 row A (slide), 1 row B, 1 row A (slide), 1 row B.

Variation 5: Alternate 2 rows B, 2 rows A, 3 rows B (slide), 2 rows A (slide), 1 row B.

Variation 6: Alternate 2 rows B, 2 rows A, 1 row B (slide), 2 rows A (slide), 3 rows B.

Variation 7: Alternate 3 rows B (slide), 1 row A, 1 row B (slide), 1 row A, 1 row B (slide), 1 row A, 1 row B (slide), 1 row A.

Variation 8: Alternate 1 row B (slide), 3 rows A, 1 row B (slide), 1 row A, 2 rows B, 2 rows A.

Variation 9: Alternate 2 rows B, 1 row A (slide), 2 rows B (slide), 1 row A, 2 rows B, 2 rows A.

Variation 10: Alternate 3 rows B (slide), 2 rows A (slide), 1 row B, 1 row A (slide), 2 rows B (slide), 1 row A.

Instructions

With A, cast on 39 sts.

Work rows 1–6 of Tweed and Solid Pattern 3 times.

Work rows 1–10 of Striped Variation 1.

Work rows 1–6 of Tweed and Solid Pattern 10 times.

Work rows 1–10 of Striped Variation 2.

Work rows 1–6 of Tweed and Solid Pattern 10 times.

Work rows 1–10 of Striped Variation 3.

Continue in this manner until all stripe patterns have been worked, then work rows 1–6 of Tweed and Solid Pattern 10 times.

Cut yarn. Weave in ends.

This project was knit with:
Artyarns Cashmere 5, 100% cashmere, 1¾ oz/50g = 102yd/39m per skein, 2 skeins color #267, 2 skeins color #239. To find equivalent yarn brands from other makers, see the Yarn Substitution Chart on page 142.

SoHo Hat

Skill Level
● ● ● ●
Intermediate

TECHNIQUE
*Two-Strand Method,
Different Sides (page 90)*

DOWNTOWN TRAIN

Finished Measurements

17"/43cm circumference x 8½"/22cm height, unstretched

Materials

Yarn: 204yd/186m of **4** medium weight yarn, cashmere

• Color A: 102yd/93m in brown

• Color B: 102yd/93m in variegated salmon and beige

Knitting needles: 5 mm (size 8 U.S.) 16"/40cm circular and double-pointed, *or size to obtain gauge*

Stitch marker

Yarn needle

Gauge

26 stitches and 20 rows = 4"/10cm in pattern stitch

Always take time to check your gauge.

Patterns

BRIM PATTERN

Rounds 1–2: *K1B, p1A, k1A, p1A; repeat from * to end of round.

Rounds 3–4: [K1B, p1B, k1A, p1B; repeat from * to end of round.

Round 5: *[K1B, p1A] 3 times, k1A, p1A; repeat from * to end of round.

HAT PATTERN

Round 6: *K1A, p1A; repeat from * to end of round.

Rounds 7–8: *K1A, p1B; repeat from * to end of round.

Round 9: *K1A, p1A; repeat from * to end of round.

Round 10: *K1B, p1A; repeat from * to end of round.

Rounds 11–12: *K1B, p1B; repeat from * to end of round.

Round 13: *K1B, p1A; repeat from * to end of round.

Instructions

With A and B held together, cast on 48 sts—total 96 single-strand stitches alternating A and B. Join to work in the round, placing a marker to identify the start of the round. Work the first round of Brim Pattern into each single-strand stitch around—96 sts. Continue with rounds 2–5 of Brim Pattern. Work Hat Pattern, repeating rounds 6–13 three times. Then repeat rounds 6–8.

DECREASE THE CROWN

See page 22 for complete instructions for decreasing in double knitting. Switch to double-pointed needles when there are too few stitches to continue on circular.

Round 1: *[K1A, p1A] 6 times, k2Atog, p2Atog; repeat from * to end of round.

Round 2: *K1B, p1A; repeat from * to end of round—84 sts.

Round 3: *[K1B, p1B] 5 times, k2Btog, p2Btog; repeat from * to end of round—72 sts.

Round 4: *K1B, p1B; repeat from * to end of round.

Round 5: *[K1B, p1A] 4 times, k2Btog, p2Atog; repeat from * to end of round—60 sts.

Round 6: *K1A, p1A; repeat from * to end of round.

Round 7: *[K1A, p1B] 3 times, k2Atog, p2Btog; repeat from * to end of round—48 sts.

Round 8: *K1A, p1B; repeat from * to end of round.

Round 9: *[K1A, p1A] twice, k2Atog, p2Atog; repeat from * to end of round—36 sts.

Round 10: *K1B, p1A; repeat from * to end of round.

Round 11: *K1B, p1B, k2Btog, p2Btog; repeat from * to end of round—24 sts.

Round 12: *K1B, p1B; repeat from * to end of round.

Round 13: *K2Btog, p2Atog; repeat from * to end of round—12 sts.

Remove the marker and cut the yarn. Thread the tail onto a yarn needle and draw it through the 12 remaining sts. Pull to tighten, secure, and weave in ends.

This project was knit with:

Artyarns Cashmere 5, 100% cashmere, 1¾ oz/50g = 102yd/93m per skein, one skein color #154, one skein color #248. To find equivalent yarn brands from other makers, see the Yarn Substitution Chart on page 142.

Bowery Trio

Skill Level
Easy

TECHNIQUE
Slip Stitch Method,
Different Sides
(page 92)

DOUBLE TAKE

Finished Measurements

Wristers: Approx 7"/18cm circumference x 9"/23cm depth, unstretched and uncuffed

Neck Warmer: Approx 16"/41cm circumference x 8"/20cm depth, unstretched

Materials

Yarn: 306yd/280m of **4** medium weight yarn, cashmere

Color A: 204yd/186m in navy

Color B: 102/93m in gray

Knitting needles: 4.5 mm (size 7 U.S.) double-pointed needles for wristers

Knitting needles: 5.5 mm (size 9 U.S.) double-pointed needles for neck warmer

Yarn needle

Gauge

18 stitches and 20 rows = 4"/10cm in Stockinette stitch

Always take time to check your gauge.

Pattern

Striped Pattern:

Round 1: With A, *[k1, sl1f] twice, k1, p1; repeat from * to end of round.

Round 2: With B, *[sl 1b, p1] twice, sl 1b, sl 1f; repeat from * to end of round.

Repeat rounds 1 and 2 for pattern.

Instructions

WRISTERS

With A and B held together and smaller needles, cast on 33 sts—66 sts on needles. Divide onto double-pointed needles and join into a round. Work Striped Pattern for 9"/23cm. Bind off in rib pattern with A.

Cut yarn, weave in ends.

NECK WARMER

Note: Both A and B are used doubled throughout.

With A and larger needles, cast on 90 st. Divide onto double-pointed needles and join into a round. Work Striped Pattern for 8"/20cm. Bind off in rib pattern with A.

Cut yarn, weave in ends.

This project was knit with:

Artyarns Cashmere 5, 100% cashmere, 1¾ oz/50g = 102yd/93m per skein, two skeins in color #267, and one skein in color #247. To find equivalent yarn brands from other makers, see the Yarn Substitution Chart on page 142.

Ribbon Candy Scarf

Skill Level
● ● ● ●
Intermediate

TECHNIQUE
*Two-Strand Method,
Similar Sides (page 91)*

102

SWEET TREAT

Finished Measurements

6"/15cm wide x 42"/107cm long

Materials

Yarn A: 326yd/298m of **3** light weight yarn, silk, in purple

Yarn B: 256yd/234m of **3** light weight yarn, silk ribbon, in variegated red and purple

Knitting needles: 3 mm (size 6 U.S.) *or size to obtain gauge*

Yarn needle

Gauge

20 stitches and 26 rows = 4"/10cm in pattern stitch

Always take time to check your gauge.

Pattern

Rows 1 and 3: *[K1A, p1B] 3 times, k1B, p1A; repeat from * 7 times, [k1A, p1B] 3 times.

Row 2: *[K1B, p1A] 3 times, k1A, p1B; repeat from * 7 times, [k1B, p1A] 3 times.

Row 4: *K1A p1B; repeat from * to end of row.

Instructions

With A, cast on 33 sts. Attach B.

Row 1 (setup row): With A and B together, k1. With A and B separately, *(k1A, p1B) into each of the next 3 stitches, (k1B, p1A) into next stitch; repeat from * 7 times, (k1A, p1B) into each of the next 3 stitches, with A and B together, k1—64 sts.

Work rows 2–4 of Pattern, working the first and last sts with A and B together as established in the setup row.

Repeat rows 1–4 of Pattern, working the first and last sts of all rows with A and B together, until scarf measures 42"/107cm or desired length, ending with row 3.

Cut B and bind off as follows: With A, k1, *k2tog, bind off; repeat from * until 1 stitch remains. Cut yarn and pull tail through last st. Weave in ends.

This project was knit with:
Artyarns Regal Silk, 100% silk, 1¾ oz/50g = 163yd/149m, 2 skeins color #235; Artyarns Silk Ribbon, 100% silk, 0.9oz/25g = 128yd/117m, in color #111. To find equivalent yarn brands from other makers, see the Yarn Substitution Chart on page 142.

Charcoal Möbius Collar

Skill Level
● ● ● ●
Intermediate

TECHNIQUE
*Two-Strand Method,
Different Sides (page 90)*

EVENING GLANCES CONNECT

Finished Measurements

32"/81cm (circumference) x 7"/18cm depth

Materials

Yarn: 400yd/366m of ③ light weight yarn, cashmere and mohair blend

- Color A: 200yd/183m in variegated brown/black
- Color B: 200yd/183m in gray

Knitting needles: 4 mm (size 6 U.S.) 40"/100cm circular, *or size to obtain gauge*

2 stitch markers in 2 different colors

Gauge

21 stitches and 24 rows = 4"/10cm in pattern stitch

Always take time to check your gauge.

Special Stitches

Pattern Stitch:

Round 1: *[K1A, p1A] 3 times, [k1B, p1B] 3 times, [K1A, p1A] 3 times, [K1B, p1B] 3 times; repeat from *.

Repeat round 1 for pattern.

DK Decrease Stitch (see page 22 for specific instructions):

Transpose the A and B stitches so that 2A and 2B can be worked together as follows: [k2tog A, p2tog B].

Instructions

With B, using Möbius cast-on (see page 18), CO 312 sts—(this will make 624 total stitches). Place marker 1 to identify start of round, and join to knit in the round.

Rounds 1–5: Attach A, and work Pattern Stitch over 5 rounds (26 times per round), slipping the marker at the end of each round.

Round 6: Work Pattern Stitch over half a round (13 times). Place marker 2 to identify decrease section. *[K1A, p1A], work DK Decrease Stitch, [k1B, p1A] 3 times; repeat from * to marker 1 (13 times).

Charcoal Möbius Collar

Rounds 7–12: Slip marker 1 and work Pattern Stitch to marker 2. Slip marker 2, then *[K1A, p1A] twice, [K1B, p1A] 3 times; repeat from * to marker 1 (13 times).

Round 13: Work Pattern Stitch over half a round (13 times). Slip marker 2, *work DK Decrease Stitch, [k1B, p1A] 3 times; repeat from * to marker 1 (13 times).

Rounds 14–20: Slip marker 1 and work Pattern Stitch to marker 2. Slip marker 2, then *K1A, p1A, [K1B, p1A] 3 times; repeat from * to marker 1 (13 times).

Bind off by working stitches as they face you, in the same order as they are worked in rounds 14–20 as follows: K1A, p1A, bind off, [k1A, bind off, p1A, bind off] twice, [k1B, bind off, p1A, bind off] 3 times, *[k1A, bind off, p1A, bind off] 3 times [k1B, bind off, p1A, bind off] 3 times; repeat from * to marker 2, remove marker, *k1A, bind off, p1A, bind off, [k1B, bind off, p1A, bind off] 3 times; repeat from * to end.

Cut yarn, weave in ends.

This project was knit with:
Artyarns Cameo, 75% cashmere, 25% mohair, 3½ oz/100g = 370yd/338m per skein, one skein color #163, and 1 skein color #2272. To find equivalent yarn brands from other makers, see the Yarn Substitution Chart on page 142.

Southport Shawl

Skill Level
● ● ● ●
Advanced

TECHNIQUES

Garter Lace Faggoting Pattern (page 60)

and Two-Strand Method, Similar Sides (page 91)

COOL SUMMER EVENING

Finished Measurements

Approximately 16½"/41.9cm wide x 45½"/115.6cm long

Materials

Yarn: 1000yd/914m of (0) lace weight yarn, cashmere

- Color A: 500yd/457m in pink
- Color B: 500yd/457m in pale melon

Knitting needles: 3.0 mm (size 6 U.S.) *or size to obtain gauge*

Gauge

20 stitches and 32 rows = 4"/10cm

Always take time to check your gauge.

Special Stitches

Lace Pattern:

*Yo, skp; repeat from * to end of row.

Lace Pattern Conversion:

With A, k1, *yo, sl 2tog, k2tog, p2sso; repeat from * to last st, k1—converted 178 sts to 90 sts.

Checkerboard Double Knit Pattern:

Row 1: K1AB, *[k1A, p1A], [k1B, p1A]; repeat from * to last st, k1AB.

Row 2: K1AB, * [k1A, p1A],[k1A, p1B]; repeat from * to last st, k1AB.

Melon Double Knit Pattern:

Row 1: K1AB, [k1B, p1A] across row to last st, k1AB.

Row 2: K1AB, [k1A, p1B] across row to last st, k1AB.

Melon Double Knit Conversion:

K1AB, [k1B, p1A] into every stitch across row to last st, k1AB—converted 90 sts to 178 sts.

Instructions

With A, cast on 90 sts.

Row 1: Work Melon Double Knit Conversion.

Rows 2–4: Work row 2, then row 1, then row 2 of Checkerboard Double Knit Pattern.

Rows 5 and 6: Work rows 1 and 2 of Melon Double Knit Pattern.

Row 7: K1AB, [k1A, p1A] twice, *k1B, p1A, [k1A, p1A] 3 times; repeat from * to last 5 sts, [k1A, p1A] twice, k1AB.

Row 8: K1AB, [k1A, p1A] twice, *k1A, p1B, [k1A, p1A] 3 times; repeat from * to last 5 sts, [k1A, p1A] twice, k1AB.

Row 9: Repeat Row 7.

Row 10: K1AB, [k1A, p1A] twice, *[k1A, p1B] 5 times, [k1A, p1A] 3 times; repeat from * to last 5 sts, [k1A, p1A] twice, k1AB.

Row 11: K1AB, [k1A, p1A] twice, *[k1B, p1A] 5 times, [k1A, p1A] 3 times; repeat from * to last 5 sts, [k1A, p1A] twice, k1AB.

Row 12: With A, work Lace Pattern Conversion—90 sts.

Rows 13 and 14: With A, k1, work Lace Pattern to last st, k1.

Rows 15 and 16: With B, k1, work Lace Pattern to last st, k1.

Rows 17 and 18: With A, k1, work Lace Pattern to last st, k1.

Row 19: Work Melon Double Knit Conversion—178 sts.

Row 20: Work Row 2 of Melon Double Knit Pattern.

Row 21: With A, work Lace Pattern Conversion—90 sts.

Rows 22–28: With A, work Lace Pattern.

Row 29: Work Melon Double Knit Conversion—178 sts.

Row 30: Work row 2 of Melon Double Knit Pattern.

Rows 31–34: Repeat rows 7–10.

Row 35: With A, work Lace Pattern Conversion—90 sts.

Rows 36–42: With A, work Lace Pattern.

Row 43: Work Melon Double Knit Conversion—178 sts.

Rows 44–46: Work rows 2, 1, and 2 of Melon Double Knit Pattern.

Rows 47 and 48: Work rows 1 and 2 of Checkerboard Double Knit Pattern.

Rows 49–51: Work rows 1, 2, and 1 of Melon Double Knit Pattern.

Row 52: With A, work Lace Pattern Conversion—90 sts.

Rows 53–66: With A, work Lace Pattern.

Row 67: Work Melon Double Knit Conversion—178 sts.

Rows 68–70: Work rows 2, 1, and 2 of Melon Double Knit Pattern.

Row 71: With A, work Lace Pattern Conversion—90 sts.

Rows 72–80: With A, work Lace Pattern.

Row 81: Work Melon Double Knit Conversion—178 sts.

Rows 82–84: Work rows 2, 1, and 2 of Melon Double Knit Pattern.

Row 85: With A, work Lace Pattern Conversion—90 sts.

Rows 86–94: With A, work Lace Pattern.

Row 95: Work Melon Double Knit Conversion—178 sts.

Rows 96 and 97: Work rows 2 and 1 of Melon Double Knit Pattern.

Rows 98 and 99: Work rows 2 and 1 of Checkerboard Double Knit Pattern.

Row 100: Work row 2 of Melon Double Knit Pattern.

Row 101: With A, work Lace Pattern Conversion—90 sts.

Rows 102–129: With A, work Lace Pattern.

Work Melon Double Knit Conversion, then beginning with row 100, work all double knit and lace sections in reverse for second half of shawl.

Cut yarn, weave in ends.

This project was knit with:
Artyarns Cashmere 1, 100% cashmere, 1¾ oz/50g = 510 yd/466m per skein, one skein color #2251, one skein color #2202. To find equivalent yarn brands from other makers, see the Yarn Substitution Chart on page 142.

Modular

USING A SERIES OF INCREASES AND DECREASES AS WELL AS PARTIAL ROWS, MODULAR PATTERNS ARE ANGLED IN VARIOUS DIRECTIONS AND KNITTED STRATEGICALLY TO BALANCE EACH OTHER, RESULTING IN A FLAT KNITTED PIECE WITH INTRIGUING GEOMETRIC SHAPES.

THE PROJECTS IN THIS CHAPTER HAVE BEEN DESIGNED TO LOOK THE SAME ON BOTH SIDES, MAKING THEM COMPLETELY WEARABLE ANY WHICH WAY. IT'S WONDERFUL NOT TO HAVE TO WORRY ABOUT WHICH SIDE FACES OUTWARD, PARTICULARLY WITH ACCESSORIES, BLANKETS, OR WRAPS. HERE YOU WILL SEE SOME SIMPLE TECHNIQUES FOR CREATING EMPHASIZING LINES IN MODULAR PATTERNS, WHETHER USING ONE YARN OR WITH MULTIPLE YARNS.

PROJECTS IN THIS CHAPTER

First Impression Scarf
Zigzag Posh Shrug
(in photo)
Paprika Shake Shawl
Shoji Wrap
Aegean Wave Afghan

MODULAR TECHNIQUES

The designs in this chapter are all based on modular short-row designs. If you have not tried them before, please refer to page 23 for an overview. Just a few hints there and you'll be on your way. Practice the simple exercises presented here to achieve modular reversibility with Garter stitch patterns.

To create an elongated stitch, double wrap a knit stitch by inserting the needle into the stitch, wrapping it twice instead of once, and pulling it through with two loops instead of one. On the return row, knit into one loop on the needle and allow the second loop to drop off to finalize the long stitch. This can be done first on one side of the work and then on the other side to ensure that the elongated stitches alternate facing to one side and then the other. This pattern can be used to emphasize groups of rows.

ABBREVIATIONS

Long St: Only work this in knit stitches—double wrap each knit stitch and pull it through with two loops on the needle.

Drop St: Knit into every long stitch just once on the return row.

Cast on 3 sts.

Row 1: K1b, inc1, sl 1f—4 sts.

Row 2: K1b, inc1, PM, k1, sl 1f—5 sts.

Row 3: K1b, k to M, RM, inc1, PM, k to last st, sl 1f.

Rows 4–7: Repeat row 3.

Row 8: K1b, Long St to M, RM, inc 1, PM, Long St to last st, sl 1f.

Row 9: K1b, Drop St to M, RM, inc 1, PM, k1, Drop St to last st, sl 1f.

Repeat rows 5–9 three more times—27 sts.

Bind off all sts. ■

Interrupted Garter Pattern in Two Colors

Attaching new colors to the opposite end of knitting, sliding the stitches from one end of the needle to the other, creates the Interrupted Garter effect, another technique for reversibility.

With A, cast on 15 sts.

Setup row: With A, k7, inc1, k1, turn; sl 1b, inc1, k2, turn; sl 1b, k1, inc1, k3, turn, sl 1b, k2, inc1, k4, turn, sl 1b, k3, inc1, k3, k2tog, k4—19 sts. Slide sts and attach B to other end of needle.

Row 1: With B, k9, inc1, k3, k2tog, k4, twist B around A (see page 21).

Row 2: With B, k8, inc1, k3, k2tog, k5, slide to other end, pick up A.

Row 3: With A, k8, inc1, k3, k2tog, k5, twist A around B.

Row 4: With A, k9, inc1, k3, k2tog, k4 slide to other end, pick up B.

Repeat rows 1–4.

On one side of the swatch, color A is emphasized, and on the other side, color B is emphasized. ■

Drop Stitch Pattern

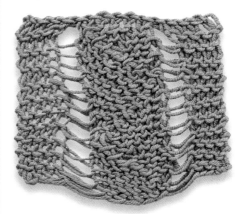

If you unravel a stitch by dropping it and letting it come apart as it is pulled down to the cast-on row, you create a "ladder" effect that looks the same on both sides. This pattern can be used to emphasize vertical multidirectional panels as well as cables.

Cast on 15 sts.

Row 1: K5, inc1, k1, turn; sl 1b, k7—16 sts.

Row 2: K5, inc1, k3, turn; sl 1b, k9—17 sts.

Row 3: K5, inc1, k5, turn; sl 1b, k11—18 sts.

Row 4: K5, inc1, k12—19 sts.

Row 5: K5, inc1, ssk, turn, sl 1b, k7.

Row 6: K5, inc1, k1, ssk, turn, sl 1b, k8.

Row 7: K5, inc1, k2, ssk, turn, sl 1b, k9.

Row 8: K5, inc1, k3, ssk, turn, sl 1b, k10.

Row 9: K5, inc1, k4, ssk, turn, sl 1b, k11.

Row 10: K5, inc1, k5, ssk, turn, sl 1b, k12.

Row 11: K5, inc1, k6, ssk, k5—19 sts.

Repeat rows 5–11 and then rows 5–7.

Next row: K9, ssk, turn; sl 1b, k4, turn; k4, ssk, turn; sl 1b, k3, turn; k3, ssk, turn; sl 1b, k2, turn; k2 ssk, turn, sl 1b, k1, turn; k to end of row.

Bind off 3, drop and unravel 1, carrying yarn to back. Knit and bind off unraveled stitch and next 5 sts, drop and unravel 1. Knit and bind off unraveled stitch and remaining 4 sts. Cut yarn. ■

Seamless modular construction refers to shapes that are created and joined to another shape at the same time. The individual pieces are not bound off, stitches are not picked up, and there is no seam on either side of the work.

Cast on 3 sts.

Row 1: K1, inc1, PM, p1.

Row 2: K to M, RM, inc1, PM, k to last st, p1.

Repeat row 2 until you have 26 sts. BO 13 sts and place last stitch back on left needle—13 sts. Place marker.

Using the knitted-on cast-on (see page 16), cast on 13 sts.

Row 1: K to st before marker, RM, k2tog, PM, k to last st, p1.

Repeat row 1 until 3 sts remain, sl 2tog, k1, p2sso.

In this example, two diamonds are joined with live stitches. The first diamond is increased and the second diamond is decreased, and the two are joined completely seamlessly. Both sides of the work are the same. There are many more ways of using seamless modular construction. The projects in this chapter all use some form of this technique. ■

First Impression Scarf

Skill Level
● ● ● ●
Easy

TECHNIQUES
Long Stitch Pattern (page 112)
and Seamless Modular
Construction (page 114)

Finished Measurements

11"/28cm wide x 58"/147cm long

Materials

Yarn: 520yd/475m of **4** medium weight yarn, silk and cashmere blend, in variegated pinks and greens

Knitting needles: 5 mm (size 8 U.S.) 24"/61cm or longer circular, *or size to obtain gauge*

Stitch marker

Stitch holder

Yarn needle

Gauge

14 stitches and 28 rows = 4"/10cm

Always take time to check your gauge.

Special Stitch

Long Stitch Pattern: Work Long Stitches into all knit stitches every 9th row. On the return (10th row), knit only the first of the double wraps for each long st, and drop the second to form the elongated stitch. Do not work Long Stitches into increased, decreased, or edge stitches.

Instructions

SET UP TRIANGLE

Cast on 3 sts.

Row 1: K1, inc1, PM, p1.

Row 2: Inc1, k to M, RM, inc1, PM, k to last st, p1.

Repeat row 2 until you have 130 stitches.

Note: Try to read your work by following instructions in The Basics, page 10, for identifying center increase shapes. Use this to double-check the marker placement and ensure you are increasing in the appropriate stitch. Eventually you'll be comfortable with identifying this stitch and can discontinue placing and removing the marker.

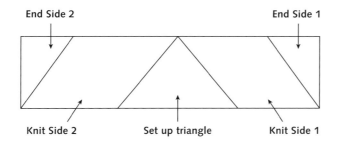

SEPARATE THE SIDES

Slide all stitches to the other end of the needle and remove half the stitches farthest away from the working yarn onto a stitch holder. Leave the other half of the stitches attached to the working yarn on the needle.

KNIT SIDE 1

Row 1: Inc1, k to last 2 sts, p2tog.

Row 2: Sl 1b, k to end of row.

Repeat rows 1–2, working a Long Stitch into every k stitch (not into p2tog or inc1 stitches) every 9th row until 8 Long Stitch Pattern rows have been created.

END SIDE 1

Bind off sts as follows:

Row 1: Sl 1b, k to last 2 sts, p2tog.

Repeat row 1, maintaining Long Stitch Pattern until 3 sts remain. Sl 1b, k2tog, psso. Cut yarn.

KNIT SIDE 2

Move stitches from holder onto needle. Attach yarn to top of center-increase triangle (opposite end of cast-on stitches). Sl 1b, k to end of row.

Row 1: Inc1, k to last 2 sts, p2tog.

Row 2: Sl 1b, k to end of row.

Repeat rows 1–2, inserting Long Stitch into every k stitch (not into p2tog or inc1 stitches) every 9th row until 8 Long Stitch Pattern rows have been created.

END SIDE 2

End as for Side 1.

Cut yarn. Weave in ends.

This project was knit with:
Artyarns Ensemble, 75% silk/25% cashmere, medium weight 2-strand yarn, 3½ oz/100g = 256yd/234m per skein, 2 skeins color #105. To find equivalent yarn brands from other makers, see the Yarn Substitution Chart on page 142.

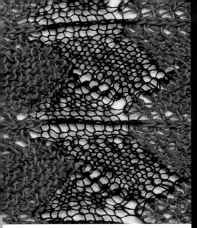

Zigzag Posh Shrug

Skill Level
● ● ● ●
Intermediate

TECHNIQUE
*Seamless Modular
Construction (page 114)*

BOLT FROM THE BLUE

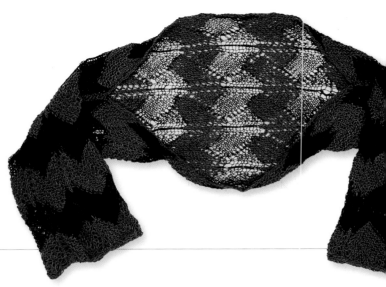

Finished Measurements

16"/41m wide x 50"/127m long

Materials

Color A: 300yd/274m of (4) medium weight yarn, silk, in teal

Color B: 300yd/274m of (0) lace weight yarn, cashmere, in deep brown

Knitting needles: 5 mm (size 8 U.S.) *or size to obtain gauge*

Medium crochet hook for edging

Gauge

16 stitches and 32 rows = 4"/10cm in Garter stitch with (4) medium weight yarn

Always take time to check your gauge.

Note: When the instructions say "turn," you literally turn the work around and head in the opposite direction. For some hints in reading your work, refer to The Basics, page 23.

Special Stitch

Lace Pattern (Lace Pat): Yo, sl 1, k2tog, psso, yo.

Instructions

With color A, cast on 47 stitches (this includes 7 stitches for each multidirectional panel and 3 stitches for each lace panel).

SHRUG SETUP

Panel 1

Inc1, k1, turn; sl 1, k2, turn.

Inc1, k3, turn; sl 1, k4, turn.

Inc1, k5, turn; sl 1, k6, turn.

Inc1, k7, turn; sl 1, k8, turn.

Inc1, k9, turn; sl 1, k10, turn.

Inc1, k11; *do not turn.*

Panels 2–5

*Lace Pat, inc1, k1, turn; sl 1, k2, Lace Pat, inc1, ssk, turn.

Sl 1, k2, Lace Pat, inc1, k3, turn; sl 1, k4, Lace Pat, inc1, k1, ssk, turn.

Sl 1, k3, Lace Pat, inc1, k5, turn; sl 1, k6, Lace Pat, inc1, k2, ssk, turn.

Sl 1, k4, Lace Pat, inc1, k7, turn; sl 1, k8, Lace Pat, inc1, k3, ssk, turn.

Sl 1, k5, Lace Pat, inc1, k9, turn; sl 1, k10, Lace Pat, inc1, k4, ssk, turn.

Sl 1, k6, Lace Pat, inc1, k11; *do not turn.*

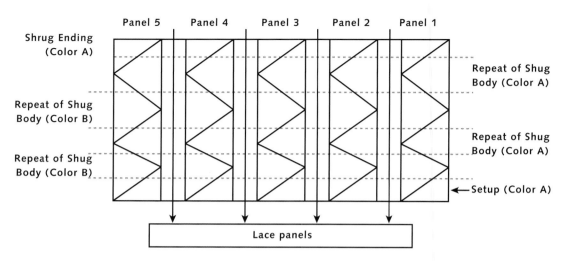

Repeat from * 3 more times (end of row).

Inc1, ssk, turn; sl 1, k2, turn.

Inc1, k1, ssk, turn; sl 1, k3, turn.

Inc1, k2, ssk, turn; sl 1, k4, turn.

Inc1, k3, ssk, turn; sl 1, k5, turn.

Inc1, k4, ssk, turn; sl 1, k6 (end of row).

Cut color A, attach color B.

SHRUG BODY

Inc1, k5, ssk, turn; sl 1, k7, turn.

Inc1, k6, ssk, turn; sl 1, k8, turn.

Inc1, k7, ssk, turn; sl 1, k9, turn.

Inc1, k8, ssk, turn; sl 1, k10, turn.

Inc1, k9, ssk, turn; sl 1, k11, turn.

Inc1, k10, ssk, *do not turn.*

*Lace Pat, inc1, k5, ssk, turn; sl 1, k7, Lace Pat, inc1, ssk, turn.

S1 1, k2, Lace Pat, inc1, k6, ssk, turn; sl 1, k8, Lace Pat, inc1, k1, ssk, turn.

S1 1, k3, Lace Pat, inc1, k7, ssk, turn; sl 1, k9, Lace Pat, inc1, k2, ssk, turn.

S1 1, k4, Lace Pat, inc1, k8, ssk, turn; sl 1, k10, Lace Pat, inc1, k3, ssk, turn.

S1 1, k5, Lace Pat, inc1, k9, ssk, turn; sl 1, k11, Lace Pat, inc1, k4, ssk, turn.

S1 1, k6, Lace Pat, inc1, k10, ssk, *do not turn.*

Repeat from * 3 more times (end of row).

Inc1, ssk, turn; sl 1, k2, turn.

Inc1, k1, ssk, turn; sl 1, k3, turn.

Inc1, k2, ssk, turn; sl 1, k4, turn.

Inc1, k3, ssk, turn; sl 1, k5, turn.

Inc1, k4, ssk, turn; sl 1, k6, turn.

Cut color B. Repeat the shrug body sequence with color A, and then alternate with between color B and color A, cutting the yarn each time, and ending with color A when shrug measures 50"/127cm from the cast-on edge.

SHRUG ENDING

With A, k6, ssk, turn; sl 1, k5, sl 1, turn.

*Sl 1, sl 1, psso, k4, ssk, turn; sl 1, k4, sl 1, turn.

Sl 1, sl 1, psso, k3, ssk, turn; sl 1, k3, sl 1, turn.

Sl 1, sl 1, psso, k2, ssk, turn; sl 1, k2, sl 1, turn.

Sl 1, sl 1, psso, k1, ssk, turn; sl 1, k1, sl 1, turn.

Sl 1, sl 1, psso, ssk; pass first st on right needle over second st.

Bind off 4, k5, ssk, turn, sl 1, k5, sl 1, turn.

Repeat from * 3 more times.

Last (5th) Repeat:

*k8, ssk, turn; sl 1, k7, s1, turn.

Sl 1, sl 1, psso, k5, ssk, turn; sl 1, k5, sl 1, turn.

Sl 1, sl 1, psso, k4, ssk, turn; sl 1, k4, sl 1, turn.

Sl 1, sl 1, psso, k3, ssk, turn; sl 1, k3, sl 1, turn.

Sl 1, sl 1, psso, k2, ssk, turn; sl 1, k2, sl 1, turn.

Sl 1, sl 1, psso, k1, ssk, turn; sl 1, k1, sl 1, turn.

Sl 1, sl 1 psso, ssk; pass first st on right needle over second st.

Cut yarn.

FINISHING

With color A, single crochet around entire border to hide all ends. Seam 20"/51m from each edge. Weave in all ends.

This project was knit with:

Artyarns Regal Silk, 100% silk, 1¾ oz/50g = 163yd/149m per skein, 3 skeins color #284.

Artyarns Cashmere 1, 100% cashmere, 1¾ oz/50g = 510yd/466m per skein, 1 skein color #268. To find equivalent yarn brands from other makers, see the Yarn Substitution Chart on page 142.

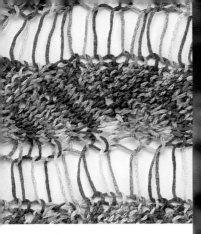

Paprika Shake Shawl

Skill Level
• • • •
Intermediate

TECHNIQUES
*Drop Stitch Pattern (page 113)
and Seamless Modular
Construction (page 114)*

SAMPLING NEW FLAVORS

Finished Measurements

15"/38cm wide x 40"/102cm long

Materials

Yarn: 340yd/311m of  light weight yarn, silk, in variegated silver and rust

Knitting needles: 5 mm (size 8 U.S.) *or size to obtain gauge*

Gauge

16 stitches and 24 rows = 4"/10cm in Garter stitch

Always take time to check your gauge.

Abbreviations

Sl 1: Slip 1 stitch purlwise with yarn in front.

Note: When the instructions say "turn," you literally turn the work around and head in the opposite direction. For some hints in reading your work, refer to The Basics, page 23.

Instructions

Cast on 43 sts.

SHAWL SETUP

Panel 1

K3, inc1, k1, turn; sl 1, p2, k3, turn.

K3, inc1, k3, turn; sl 1, p4, k3, turn.

K3, inc1, k5, turn; sl 1, p6, k3, turn.

K3, inc1, k7, *do not turn.*

Panel 2

*K3, inc1, k1, turn; sl 1, p2, k3, inc1, ssk, turn.

Sl 1, p2, k3, inc1, k3, turn; sl 1, p4, k3, inc1, k1, ssk, turn.

S l 1, p3, k3, inc1, k5, turn; sl 1, p6, k3, inc1, k2, ssk, turn.

S l 1, p4, k3, inc1, k7, *do not turn.*

Repeat from * twice more for Panels 3 and 4.

Panel 5

Repeat from * in Panel 2, k3 (end of row).

K3, inc1, ssk, turn; sl 1, p2, k3, turn.

K3, inc1, k1, ssk, turn; sl 1, p3, k3, turn.

K3, inc1, k2, ssk, turn; sl 1, p4, k3—63 sts.

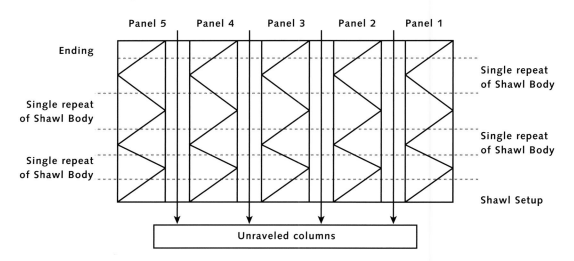

SHAWL BODY

K3, inc1, k3, ssk, turn; sl 1, p5, k3, turn.

K3, inc1, k4, ssk, turn; sl 1, p6, k3, turn.

K3, inc1, k5, ssk, turn; sl 1, p7, k3, turn.

K3, inc1, k6, ssk, *do not turn.*

*K3, inc1, k3, ssk, turn; sl 1, p5, k3, inc1, ssk, turn.

Sl 1, p2, k3, inc1, k4, ssk, turn; sl 1, p6, k3, inc1, k1, ssk, turn.

Sl 1, p3, k3, inc1, k5, ssk, turn; sl 1, p7, k3, inc1, k2, ssk, turn.

Sl 1, p4, k3, inc1, k6, ssk, *do not turn.*

Repeat from * 3 more times, k3 (end of row).

K3, inc1, ssk, turn; sl 1, p2, k3, turn.

K3, inc1, k1, ssk, turn; sl 1, p3, k3, turn.

K3, inc1, k2, ssk, turn; sl 1, p4, k3, turn.

Repeat the Shawl Body sequence until shawl measures 40"/102cm from the cast-on edge.

SHAWL ENDING

Bind off 3 sts.

*K3, ssk, turn; sl 1, p3, s1, turn.

Sl 1, sl 1, psso, k2, ssk, turn; sl 1, p2, sl 1, turn.

Sl 1, sl 1, psso, k1, ssk; turn; sl 1, p1, sl 1, turn.

Sl 1, sl 1, psso, ssk; pass first st on right needle over second st.

Bind off 1.

Drop the next stitch to unravel, pick up a stitch by knitting into the bar, and bind off (pass previous stitch over stitch just knitted); drop the next stitch to unravel, pick up a stitch by purling into the bar, and bind off (pass previous stitch over stitch just purled); bind off 1.

Repeat from * 3 more times.

Last (5th) Repeat:

K3, ssk, turn; sl 1, p3, sl 1, turn.

Sl 1, sl 1, psso, k2, ssk, turn; sl 1, p2, sl 1, turn.

Sl 1, sl 1, psso, k1, ssk turn; sl 1, p1, sl 1, turn.

Sl 1, sl 1, psso, ssk; pass first st on right needle over second st, bind off 3.

Cut yarn and pull through remaining stitch. Weave in ends.

This project was knit with:
Artyarns Silk Pearl, 100% silk, light weight yarn, 1¾oz/50g = 170yd/155m per skein, 2 skeins color #175. To find equivalent yarn brands from other makers, see the Yarn Substitution Chart on page 142.

Shoji
Wrap

Skill Level
● ● ● ●
Intermediate

TECHNIQUE
*Seamless Modular
Construction (page 114)*

DELICATE TOUCH

Finished Measurements

22"/56cm wide x 49"/124cm from front edge to back point

Materials

Yarn: 1020yd/933m of (**0**) lace weight yarn, cashmere, in variegated gray and khaki; 115yd/105m of (**3**) light weight yarn, cashmere/silk with beads, in variegated gray and khaki (optional for trim)

Knitting needles: 4 mm (size 6 U.S.) *or size to obtain gauge*

Small crochet hook

Gauge

16 stitches and 32 rows = 4"/10cm in Pattern Stitch

Always take time to check your gauge.

Special Stitch

Lace Pattern (LP): Yo, sl 2tog, k1, p2sso, yo.

LACE PATTERN RULES

• When increasing in pattern, a new Lace Pattern should be added every time there are 6 stitches between the last Lace Pattern and the edge stitches or center stitches. Edge stitches are defined as the [k1] at the beginning of the row and the [p1] at the end of the row. Center stitches are the [inc1] at the center of each row.

• When decreasing in pattern, discontinue working a Lace Pattern when there are not enough stitches to work the full 3-stitch motif, and knit these stitches instead. For example, if there are only 2 stitches left before a [k2tog] or [p2tog], but the pattern as set would dictate that a Lace Pattern should be worked, knit the 2 stitches instead.

• There should always be 3 knit stitches between Lace Patterns, except when you're adding new LPs on either side of the center stitch—then there's LP, inc1, LP, followed by LP, k1, inc1, k1, LP, followed by LP, k2, inc1, k2, LP, and so on.

• Lace Patterns should line up vertically. The [sl 2tog, k1, p2sso] of a Lace Pattern should be directly above the [sl 2tog, k1, p2sso] of the Lace Pattern worked on the previous odd-numbered row.

Instructions

DIAMOND 1

Cast on 3 sts.

Row 1: K1, inc1, p1.

Row 2: K1, inc1, k1, p1.

Row 3: K2, inc1, k1, p1.

Row 4: K2, inc1, k2, p1.

Row 5: K3, inc1, k2, p1.

Row 6: K3, inc1, k3, p1.

Row 7: K1, LP, inc1, PM, LP, p1.

Row 8: K4, RM, inc1, PM, k4, p1.

Row 9: K1, LP to M, RM, inc1, PM, LP to last st, p1.

Row 10: K1, k to M, RM, inc1, PM, k to last st, p1.

Repeat rows 9 and 10 until you have 150 sts. Remove marker. Divide the sts in half, transferring 75 sts farthest from the working yarn to stitch holder.

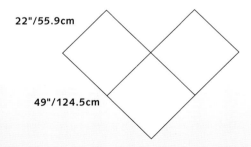

22"/55.9cm

49"/124.5cm

DIAMOND 2

Using the knitted-on cast-on (see p 000), place marker, cast on an additional 75 sts—150 sts on needle, 75 sts on stitch holder.

Row 1: K1, LP to M, RM, k2tog, PM, LP to last st, p1.

Row 2: K to M, RM, k2tog, PM, k to last st, p1.

Repeat rows 1 and 2 until 3 sts remain. Sl 2tog, k1, p2sso. Cut yarn, weave in ends.

Chart legend:

- ☐ Knit
- ☒ Knit
- ⚊ (∧) sl 2tog, k1, psso
- Ⓞ Yarn over
- ☑ (V) Inc1

DIAMOND 3

Transfer sts from holder to needle. Repeat instructions for Diamond 2.

Finishing

Using crochet hook and Yarn B, single-crochet around entire edge. Cut yarn. Weave in ends.

This project was knit with:

Artyarns Cashmere 1, 100% cashmere, lace weight yarn, 1¾ oz/50g = 510yd/466m per skein, 2 skeins color #159; Artyarns Beaded Cashmere, 50% cashmere/50% silk strand with gold glass beads, 1¾ oz/50g = 115yd/105m per skein, 1 skein color #159. To find equivalent yarn brands from other makers, see the Yarn Substitution Chart on page 142.

Aegean Wave Afghan

Skill Level
● ● ● ●
Intermediate

TECHNIQUES
*Interrupted Garter Pattern
in Two Colors
(page 113)*

*and Seamless Modular
Construction
(page 114)*

Finished Measurements

26"/66cm wide x 68"/173cm long

Materials

Yarn: Approx 1326yd/1212m of medium weight yarn, cashmere

- Color A: 204yd/187m in teal
- Color B: 204yd/187m in blue-green
- Color C: 306yd/280m in lime green
- Color D: 204yd/187m in blue
- Color E: 204yd/187m in dark blue
- Color F: 204yd/187m in variegated blues

Knitting needles: 5.5 mm (size 9 U.S.) 29"/74cm circular *or size to obtain gauge*

Stitch markers

Gauge

16 stitches and 28 rows = 4"/10cm in Garter stitch
Always take time to check your gauge.

Special Stitches

Rib Panel:

*K1, p1; repeat from * 4 more times.

Upright Chevron:

K17, yo, k17, k2tog—36 sts.

V Chevron:

Inc1, k 18, k2tog, k17—38 sts

Blanket Pattern:

Work rows as follows: Rib Panel, Upright Chevron, Rib Panel, V Chevron, Rib Panel, Upright Chevron, Rib Panel

Instructions

With A, cast on 98 sts.

SETUP

With A, work Rib Panel over 10 sts, k9, yo, k1, yo, k1, turn; sl 1, k4, turn.

Sl 1, k1, yo, k1, yo, k3, turn; sl 1, k8, turn.

Sl 1, k3, yo, k1, yo, k5, turn; sl 1, k12, turn.

Sl 1, k5, yo, k1, yo, k7, turn; sl 1, k16, turn.

Sl 1, k7, yo, k1, yo, k9, turn; sl 1, k20, turn.

Sl 1, k9, yo, k1, yo, k11, turn; sl 1, k24, turn.

Sl 1, k11, yo, k1, yo, k13, turn; sl 1, k28, turn.

Sl 1, k13, yo, k1, yo, k15, turn; sl 1, k32, turn.

Sl 1, k15, yo, k1, yo, k17, turn; sl 1, k34, k2tog, work Rib Panel (end of row).

Aegean Wave Afghan

Row 1: Rib Panel, Upright Chevron, Rib Panel, PM1, inc1, k1, turn; PM2, sl 1, k2, Rib Panel, Upright Chevron.

Row 2: Rib Panel, Upright Chevron, Rib Panel, sm1, inc1, k to M2, RM2, k1, turn; PM2, sl 1, k to Marker 1, sm1, Rib Panel, Upright Chevron, Rib Panel (end of row).

Repeat row 2 until there are 19 stitches between markers 1 and 2. Cut yarn.

At this point, 75 stitches have been worked and 49 cast-on stitches remain.

Slide stitches to the other end of the needle, attach A, repeat setup as for first half. Do not cut yarn. You have 150 stitches on the needles.

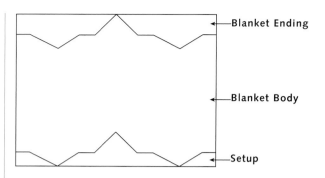

BLANKET BODY

Slide stitches to the other end of the needle. Attach B.

Rows 1 and 2: With B, work 2 rows of Blanket Pattern. Slide stitches to other end of needle.

Rows 3 and 4: Carry A up and work 2 rows of Blanket Pattern. Slide stitches to other end of needle.

Rows 5 and 6: Repeat rows 1 and 2.

Rows 7 and 8: Repeat rows 3 and 4.

Rows 9 and 10: Repeat rows 1 and 2.

Rows 11 and 12: Repeat rows 3 and 4.

Cut A, slide sts to the other end of the needle.

Rows 13–20: With B, work 8 rows of Blanket Pattern.

Repeat the blanket body sequence, sliding stitches and adding new colors on the opposite side, in the following order: C, D, E, F, C, F, E, D, C, B.

Note: When adding a new color, always slide the stitches to other side of needle to add and work rows 1–12 alternating between the new color and the previous color.

BLANKET ENDING

Attach A.

Row 1: With A, work Rib Stitch, k17, sl 1, turn; sl 1, sl 1, psso, k14, k2tog, work Rib Stitch.

Row 2: Work Rib Stitch, k15, sl 1, turn; sl 1, sl 1, psso, k12, k2tog, work Rib Stitch.

Row 3: Work Rib Stitch, k13, sl 1, turn; sl 1, sl 1, psso, k10, k2tog, work Rib Stitch.

Row 4: Work Rib Stitch, k11, sl 1, turn; sl 1, sl 1, psso, k8, k2tog, work Rib Stitch.

Row 5: Work Rib Stitch, k9, sl 1, turn; sl 1, sl 1, psso, k6, k2tog, work Rib Stitch.

Row 6: Work Rib Stitch, k7, sl 1, turn; sl 1, sl 1, psso, k4, k2tog, work Rib Stitch.

Row 7: Work Rib Stitch, k5, sl 1, turn; sl 1, sl 1, psso, k2, k2tog, work Rib Stitch.

Row 8: Work Rib Stitch, k3, sl 1, turn; sl 1, sl 1, psso, k2tog, work Rib Stitch.

Row 9: Bind off all stitches you've worked with color A, cut yarn.

Slide stitches to the other end of the needle, attach A, and repeat instructions as above.

To finish the center, attach A and proceed as follows:

Row 1: K16, k2tog, Rib Stitch, V Chevron, Rib Stitch, k 17, sl 1.

Row 2: Sl 1, sl 1, psso, k15, k2tog, Rib Stitch, V Chevron, Rib Stitch, k16, sl 1.

Row 3: Sl 1, sl 1, psso, k13, k2tog, Rib Stitch, V Chevron, Rib Stitch, k16, sl 1.

Row 4: Sl 1, sl 1, psso, k13, k2tog, Rib Stitch, V Chevron, Rib Stitch, k14, sl 1.

Row 5: Sl 1, sl 1, psso, k11, k2tog, Rib Stitch, V Chevron, Rib Stitch, k14, sl 1.

Row 6: Sl 1, sl 1, psso, k11, k2tog, Rib Stitch, V Chevron, Rib Stitch, k12, sl 1.

Row 7: Sl 1, sl 1, psso, k9, k2tog, Rib Stitch, V Chevron, Rib Stitch, k12, sl 1.

Row 8: Sl 1, sl 1, psso, k9, k2tog, Rib Stitch, V Chevron, Rib Stitch, k10, sl 1.

Row 9: Sl 1, sl 1, psso, k7, k2tog, Rib Stitch, V Chevron, Rib Stitch, k10, sl 1.

Row 10: Sl 1, sl 1, psso, k7, k2tog, Rib Stitch, V Chevron, Rib Stitch, k8, sl 1.

Row 11: Sl 1, sl 1, psso, k5, k2tog, Rib Stitch, V Chevron, Rib Stitch, k8, sl 1.

Row 12: Sl 1, sl 1, psso, k5, k2tog, Rib Stitch, V Chevron, Rib Stitch, k6, sl 1.

Row 13: Sl 1, sl 1, psso, k3, k2tog, Rib Stitch, V Chevron, Rib Stitch, k6, sl 1.

Row 14: Sl 1, sl 1, psso, k3, k2tog, Rib Stitch, V Chevron, Rib Stitch, k4, sl 1.

Row 15: Sl 1, sl 1, psso, k1, k2tog, Rib Stitch, V Chevron, Rib Stitch, k4, sl 1.

Row 16: Sl 1, sl 1, psso, k1, k2tog, Rib Stitch, V Chevron, Rib Stitch, k2, sl 1.

Row 17: Sl 1, sl 1, psso, k1, psso, Rib Stitch, V Chevron, Rib Stitch, k2, sl 1.

Row 18: Sl 1, sl 1, psso, k1, psso, bind off 10 Rib Stitches, k19, k2tog, k17, Rib Stitch, turn; bind off 10 Rib Stitches, bind off 1, k16, k2tog, k16, sl 1.

Row 19: Sl 1, sl 1, psso, k15, k2tog, k15, sl 1.

Row 20: Sl 1, sl 1, psso, k14, k2tog, k14, sl 1.

Row 21: Sl 1, sl 1, psso, k13, k2tog, k13, sl 1.

Row 22: Sl 1, sl 1, psso, k12, k2tog, k12, sl 1.

Row 23: Sl 1, sl 1, psso, k11, k2tog, k11, sl 1.

Row 24: Sl 1, sl 1, psso, k10, k2tog, k10, sl 1.

Row 25: Sl 1, sl 1, psso, k9, k2tog, k9, sl 1.

Row 26: Sl 1, sl 1, psso, k8, k2tog, k8, sl 1.

Row 27: Sl 1, sl 1, psso, k7, k2tog, k7, sl 1.

Row 28: Sl 1, sl 1, psso, k6, k2tog, k6, sl 1.

Row 29: Sl 1, sl 1, psso, k5, k2tog, k5, sl 1.

Row 30: Sl 1, sl 1, psso, k4, k2tog, k4, sl 1.

Row 31: Sl 1, sl 1, psso, k3, k2tog, k3, sl 1.

Row 32: Sl 1, sl 1, psso, k2, k2tog, k2, sl 1.

Row 33: Sl 1, sl 1, psso, k1, k2tog, k1, sl 1.

Row 34: Sl 1, sl 1, psso, bind off 4 sts.

Cut yarn. Weave in ends.

This project was knit with:
Artyarns Cashmere 5, 100% cashmere, medium weight 5-strand yarn, 1¾ oz/50g = 102yd/93m per skein; 3 skeins of color C, #217; 2 skeins each of colors A, #230; B, #204; D, #228; E, # 207; and F, #107. To find equivalent yarn brands from other makers, see the Yarn Substitution Chart on page 142.

MORE
Techniques
TO
EXPLORE

I'VE INCLUDED A GROUP OF SWATCHES IN THIS SECTION TO INSPIRE YOU TO BUILD ON THE TECHNIQUES THAT YOU HAVE LEARNED IN THIS BOOK. THE COMBINATIONS YOU CAN CREATE IN REVERSIBLE KNITTING ARE ENDLESS, AND HERE ARE JUST SOME OF THE POSSIBILITIES. IT IS HELPFUL TO REFER TO THE CHARTS INCLUDED AT THE END OF THE CHAPTER FOR MOST OF THESE SWATCHES, BECAUSE THEY WILL TEACH BY EXAMPLE HOW YOU CAN CHART YOUR OWN ADVANCED DESIGNS.

IN THIS CHAPTER

Mixed Cables

Wavy Design

Nine Squares

Knit and Purl in Double Knitting

Cables in Colors

Angular Embossed Knitting

MASTER MORE METHODS

ONLINE!
Explore more of my exclusive bonus content online at **www.larkcrafts.com/bonus**

Written instructions, keyed charts, and video show you how!

Mixed Cables

chart on page 139

These swatches show two different sides with cables, using 2x2 rib and 2-stranded double knitting. As you can see, double knitting does not have to use 1x1 rib, although that is most common. This example shows a 2x2 rib for double knitting with cables. Each side of the fabric is worked independently, but the end result is a double-thick fabric with different patterns on each side.

To make the chart easy to read, the rows for the two sides have been put on separate charts, and a blank line is left between each row. Work Row 1 from the first chart, then turn the work and follow Row 2 from the second chart.

All odd-numbered rows are read from right to left and even-numbered rows are read from left to right.

Abbreviations

C2/2/2F: Transfer 2 sts to cn1 and hold in front of work, transfer 2 sts to cn2 and hold in back of work, k2, p2 from cn2, k2 from cn1. (Follow color patterning as specified.)

C2/2/2B: Transfer 2 sts to cn1 and hold in back of work, transfer 2 sts to cn2 and hold in back of cn1, k2 from left needle, transfer sts from cn1 to left needle, transfer sts from cn2 to left needle, p2, k2. (Follow color patterning as specified.)

With A, cast on 50 sts. Attach B.

Row 1: K1B, [p2A, k2B] 2 times, p2B, (k2A, p2B) 3 times, [C2/2/2B—ABA], p2B, [k2A, p2B] 2 times, k2A, [p2A, k2B] 2 times, k1B.

Row 2: K1A, [p2B, k2A] 2 times, p2B, [C2/2/2B—BAB], p2A, [k2B, p2A] 4 times, [C2/2/2/F—BAB], [p2B, k2A] 2 times, k1A.

Row 3: K1B, [p2A, k2B] 2 times, p2B, [k2A, p2B] 2 times, [C2/2/2B—ABA], p2B, [C2/2/2F—ABA], (p2B, k2A) 2 times, [p2A, k2B] 2 times, k1B.

Row 4: K1A, [p2B, k2A] 2 times, p2A, k2B, p2A, [C2/2/2B—BAB], p2A, [k2B, p2A] 2 times, [C2/2/2F—BAB], p2A, k2B, [p2B, k2A] 2 times, k1A.

Row 5: K1B, [p2A, k2B] 2 times, p2B, k2A, p2B, [C2/2/2B—ABA], p2B, [k2B, p2B] 2 times, [C2/2/2F—ABA], p2B, k2A, [p2A, k2B] 2 times, k1B.

Row 6: Repeat Row 2.

Row 7: K1B, [p2A, k2B] 2 times, p2B, [C2/2/2B—ABA], p2B, k2A, [p2B, k2B] 2 times, p2B, k2A, p2B, [C2/2/2F—ABA], [p2A, k2B] 2 times, k1B.

Row 8: Repeat Row 4.

Row 9: K1B, [p2A, k2B] 2 times, p2B, [C2/2/2F—ABA], p2B, k2A, [p2B, k2B] 2 times, p2B, k2A, p2B, [C2/2/2B—ABA], [p2A, k2B] 2 times, k1B.

Row 10: Repeat Row 2.

Row 11: K1B, [p2A, k2B] 2 times, p2B, k2A, p2B, [C2/2/2F—ABA], p2B, [k2A, p2B] 2 times, [C2/2/2B—ABA], p2B, k2A, [p2A, k2B] 2 times, k1B.

Row 12: Repeat Row 4.

Row 13: Repeat Row 5.

Row 14: Repeat Row 2.

Row 15: Repeat Row 7.

Row 16: Repeat Row 4.

Row 17: Repeat Row 9.

Row 18: Repeat Row 2.

Row 19: Repeat Row 11.

Row 20: Repeat Row 4.

Row 21: K1B, [p2A, k2B] 2 times, p2B, [k2A, p2B] 2 times, [C2/2/2F—ABA], p2B, [C2/2/2B—ABA], [p2B, k2A] 2 times, [p2A, k2B] 2 times, k1B.

Row 22: Repeat Row 2.

Row 23: Repeat Row 1.

Row 24: Repeat Row 4.

Wavy Design

chart on page 140

This is a reversible version of a popular short row wave pattern that is found in stitch guides. Both sides are identical. The traditional Stockinette Stitch has been changed to a 1x1 Rib, and a Garter Stitch row is incorporated wherever there are color changes for additional definition. Wrapping and turning are used to prevent holes in the knitting caused by turning midstream in traditional horizontal knitting.

Abbreviations

WT (wrap and turn): Bring the yarn to the front, transfer the next stitch from the lef needle to the right needle, turn the work, bring the yarn back between the needles, and transfer that same stitch back to right needle (it is now wrapped). You will now knit in the other direction.

K1 picking up wrap: To work a wrapped stitch, place the right needle under the wrap and knit it together with the wrapped stitch.

Wave Pat: [K1, p1] 5 times, WT; [k1, p1] 4 times, WT; [k1, p1] 3 times, WT; [k1, p1] 3 times.

Multiple of 16+6 sts.

Cast on 38 sts.

Row 1: With A, [k1, p1] 8 times, WT; work Wave Pat, [k1 picking up wrap, p1] 2 times, [k1, p1] 7 times, WT; work Wave Pat, [k1 picking up wrap, p1] 2 times, [k1, p1] 2 times.

Row 2: With A, [k1, p1] 7 times, [k1 picking up wrap, p1] 2 times, [k1, p1] 6 times, [k1 picking up wrap, p1] 2 times, [k1, p1] 2 times.

Rows 3–4: With A, knit.

Row 5: With B, [k1, p1] 3 times, WT; [k1, p1] 3 times, turn; [k1, p1] 2 times, WT; (k1, p1) 2 times, turn; [k1, p1] 2 times, [k1 picking up wrap, p1] 2 times, [k1, p1] 8 times, WT; work Wave Pat, [k1 picking up wrap, p1] 2 times, [k1, p1] 6 times, turn; [k1, p1] 3 times, WT; [k1, p1] 3 times, turn; [k1, p1] 2 times, WT; [k1, p1] 2 times.

Row 6: [K1, p1] 2 times, [k1 picking up wrap, p1] 2 times, [k1, p1] 7 times, [k1 picking up wrap, p1] 2 times, [k1, p1] 6 times.

Rows 7–8: With B, knit.

Repeat Rows 1–8 for pattern.

Nine Squares

chart on page 140

Both sides of this swatch are the same but in opposite colors. Using lace and double knitting within rows as well as between rows is only possible when using the two-stranded form of double knitting. Try it with finer weight yarn for a lovely two-sided design. All of the rows for this swatch are on one chart. Read odd-numbered rows from right to left and even-numbered rows from left to right.

Abbreviation

LP (Lace Pattern): Yo, sl 2tog, k1, p2sso, yo.

With A, cast on 38 sts.

Row 1: Attach B. With B, k1, [(k1B, p1A) 5 times, work LP] 2 times, [k1B, p1A] 5 times, k1B.

Row 2: K1A, [(k1A, p1B) 5 times, work LP] 2 times, [k1A, p1B] 5 times, k1A.

Row 3: K1B, [k1B, p1A, (k1A, p1B) 3 times, k1B, p1A, work LP] 2 times, k1B, p1A, (k1A, p1B) 3 times, k1B, p1A, k1B.

Row 4: K1A, [k1A, p1B, (k1B, p1A) 3 times, k1A, p1B, work LP] 2 times, k1A, p1B, (k1B, p1A) 3 times, k1A, p1B, k1A.

Row 5: Repeat Row 1.

Row 6: Repeat Row 2.

Row 7: Drop B. With A, k1, *yo, skp; repeat from * to last st, k1.

Row 8: Knit.

Rows 9–14: Repeat Rows 1–6, substituting A for B, and B for A.

Rows 15 and 16: Repeat Rows 7 and 8.

Rows 17–22: Repeat Rows 1–6 as written.

With A, bind off all sts.

Knit and Purl in Double Knitting

Thus far we've worked double knitting so that the stitches on the side facing us are knit stitches and the stitches for the back of the fabric are purl stitches. It is possible, however, to work both knit and purl on the same side in double knitting. If you're working a row in which A is the front of the fabric and B is the back and you want to work purl stitches (i.e., p1A, k1), simply separate the two strands so that B is in back of the work (between the 2 needles) and A is in front of the work. Then purl with A. Keeping the strands in the same position, knit with B. For knit stitches, follow the instructions for double knitting on page 20, in which case you would carry both strands to the back to knit with one of them, and bring both strands to the front to purl with one of them.

With A, cast on 32 sts.

Row 1: K1A, [(k1A, p1B) 3 times, (p1A, k1B) 3 times] twice, [k1A, p1B] 3 times, k1A.

Row 2: K1B, [(k1B, p1A) 3 times, (p1B, k1A) 3 times] twice, [k1B, p1A] 3 times, k1B.

Rows 3 and 4: Repeat rows 1 and 2.

Row 5: K1A, (k1A, p1B) 15 times, k1A.

Row 6: K1B, [(p1A, k1B) 3 times, (k1A, p1B) 3 times] twice, [p1A, k1B] 3 times, k1B.

Row 7: K1A, [(p1B, k1A) 3 times, (k1B, p1A) 3 times] twice, [p1B, k1A] 3 times, k1A.

Rows 8 and 9: Repeat rows 6 and 7.

Row 10: K1B, (k1A, p1B) 15 times, k1B.

Rows 11–14: Repeat Rows 1–4.

Bind off all stitches with A.

Cables in Colors

chart on page 141

Here's an example of how to chart two-color cables that are different on each side. To make the chart easy to read, I have placed the rows for the two sides on separate charts, leaving a blank line between each row. Work Row 1 from the first chart, then turn the work and follow Row 2 from the second chart. All odd-numbered rows are read from right to left and even-numbered rows are read from left to right. It is easier to track complex designs such as this one by charting them. Two-stranded double-knitting is used throughout, so when knitting with one color remember to bring both strands to back, and when purling with one color remember to bring both strands to front.

Abbreviations

C2/2/2F: Transfer 2 sts to cn1 and hold in front of work, transfer 2 sts to cn2 and hold in back of work, k2, p2 from cn2, k2 from cn1. (Follow color patterning as specified.)

C2/2/2B: Transfer 2 sts to cn1 and hold in back of work, transfer 2 sts to cn2 and hold in back of cn1, k2 from left needle, transfer sts from cn1 to left needle, transfer sts from cn2 to left needle, p2, k2. (Follow color patterning as specified.)

With A, cast on 40 sts.

Row 1: Attach B. K1B, [k2A, p2B], [k2B, p2A], [C2/2/2F—BBA], p2A, [k2B, p2B], [k2B, p2A], [C2/2/2B—ABB], p2A, [k2B, p2B], k2A, k1B.

Row 2: K1A, p2A, [C2/2/2F—ABB], p2B, [C2/2/2F—AAB], p2B, [C2/2/2F—ABB], p2A, [C2/2/2F—ABB], p2B, [k2B, p2A], k1A.

Row 3: K1B, [C2/2/2F—BBA], p2B, [k2B, p2A], [C2/2/2F—BBA], p2A, [C2/2/2B—ABB], p2A, [k2B, p2B], [C2/2/2B—AAB], k1B.

Row 4: K1A, p2B, [k2A, p2A], [C2/2/2F—ABB], p2B, [C2/2/2F—AAB], p2A, [C2/2/2F—ABB], p2B, [C2/2/2F—AAB], p2B, k1A

Row 5: K1B, [k2B, p2B], [C2/2/2F—BAA], p2B, [k2B, p2A], [C2/2/2F—ABA], p2A, [k2B, p2B], [C2/2/2B—AAB], p2A, k2B, k1B.

Row 6: K1A, p2B, [C2/2/2F—BBA], p2A, [C2/2/2F—ABB], p2A, [C2/2/2F—AAB], p2B, [C2/2/2F—AAB], p2B, [k2B, p2B], k1A.

Row 7: K1B, [k2B, p2B], [k2B, p2B], [C2/2/2F—BAA], p2B, [k2A, p2A], [k2A, p2B], [C2/2/2B—AAB], p2A, [k2B, p2B], k2B, k1B.

Row 8: K1A, p2B, [k2B, p2B], [C2/2/2F—BBA], p2A, [C2/2/2F—AAB], p2A, [C2/2/2F—ABB], p2B, k1A.

Row 9: K1B, [k2B, p2B], [k2B, p2A], [k2B, p2B], [C2/2/2F—AAA], p2B, [C2/2/2B—AAA], p2A, [k2B, p2B], [k2B, p2B], k2B, k1B.

Row 10: K1A, p2B, [C2/2/2F—BBB], p2B, [C2/2/2F—BAA], p2A, [C2/2/2F—AAB], p2A, [C2/2/2F—ABB], p2B, [k2B, p2B], k1A.

Row 11: K1B, [k2B, p2B], [k2B, p2B], [K2B, p2A], [k2A, p2B], [C2/2/2F—AAA], p2A, [k2A, p2B], [k2B, p2B], [k2B, p2B], k2B, k1B.

Row 12: K1A, p2B, [k2B, p2B], [C2/2/2F—ABB], p2A, [C2/2/2F—BAA], p2A, [C2/2/2F—AAB], p2B, [C2/2/2F—ABB], p2B, k1A.

Row 13: K1B, [k2B, p2B], [k2B, p2A], [C2/2/2B—ABB], p2A, [k2A, p2A], [k2A, p2B], [C2/2/2F—BBA], p2A, [k2B, p2B], k2B, k1B.

Row 14: K1A, p2B, [C2/2/2F—BBB], p2A, [C2/2/2F—ABB], p2A, [C2/2/2F—BAA], p2B, [C2/2/2F—AAB], p2B, [k2B, p2B], k1A.

Row 15: K1B, k2B, p2B, [C2/2/2B—ABB], p2A, [k2B, p2A], [C2/2/2F—ABA], p2B, [k2B, p2A], [C2/2/2F—BBA], p2B, k2B, k1B.

Row 16: K1A, p2B, [k2B, p2A], [C2/2/2F—ABB], p2B, [C2/2/2F—AAB], p2A, [C2/2/2F—BBA], p2B, [C2/2/2F—AAB], p2B, k1A.

Row 17: K1B, [C2/2/2B—ABB], p2A, [k2B, p2B], [C2/2/2B—ABB], p2A, [C2/2/2F—BBA], p2A, [k2B, p2B], [C2/2/2F—BBA], k1B.

Row 18: K1A, p2A, [C2/2/2F—BBB], p2B, [C2/2/2F—AAB], p2B, [C2/2/2F—ABB], p2A, [C2/2/2F—BBA], p2B, [k2B, p2A], k1A.

Row 19: K1B, [k2A, p2B], [k2B, p2A], [k2B, p2B], [k2A, p2B], [k2B, p2A], [k2B, p2B], [K2A, p2A], [k2B, p2B], [k2B, p2B], k2B, k1B.

Row 20: K1A, p2B, [k2B, p2B], [C2/2/2F—ABB], p2A, [C2/2/2F—ABB], p2B, [C2/2/2F—AAB], p2B, [C2/2/2F—BBA], p2A, k1A.

Row 21: K1B, [k2A, p2A], [k2B, p2B], [C2/2/2B—ABB], p2A, [k2B, p2B], [k2B, p2A], [C2/2/2F—BAA], p2A, [k2B, p2B], k2A, k1B.

Row 22: K1A, p2A, [C2/2/2F—BBA], p2B, [C2/2/2F—AAB], p2B, [C2/2/2F—ABB], p2A, [C2/2/2F—BBA], p2B, [k2A, p2A], k1A.

Row 23: K1B, [k2A, p2A], [C2/2/2B—BAA], p2B, [k2B, p2B], [k2B, p2A], [k2B, p2B], [k2B, p2A], [C2/2/2F—AAB], p2B, k2A, k1B.

Bind off all stitches with A.

Angular Embossed Knitting

Embossed Knitting is a term I coined to describe the process of adding stitches on one side of the fabric that layer over the knitted piece but do not affect its shape or construction. In this example, I've added embossed knitting with one of the two strands used together, and the decorative layer is only seen on one side. The additional stitches are removed prior to the bind-off. Because they layer over one side, they do not affect the gauge, width, or length of the piece.

Abbreviation

K1/2e: Knit 1 with AB and make 2 extra stitches with B alone the first time this abbreviation is used as follows: With AB together, k1 stitch, but do not remove from left needle, then with only B, knit into the back of the stitch, and then again into the front of the stitch, bringing up 2 extra loops with B—total 3 sts. On subsequent rows, if the 2e stitches are already there, just knit them.

Note: Two strands are worked together throughout, except where "e" stitches are specified, in which case only B is worked. When purling e stitches, bring yarn A to the front.

Cast on 3 sts with A and B.

Row 1: K1, inc1, p1—4 sts

Row 2: Inc1, inc1, k1, p1—6 sts

Row 3: Inc1, k1, inc1, k2, p1—8 sts

Row 4: Inc1, [k1/2e] 2 times, inc1, pm, [k1/2e] 2 times, k1, p1

Rows 5, 7, 9: Inc1, k to marker, purling all e sts, rm, inc1, pm, k to last st, purling all e sts, p1.

Row 6: Inc1, k1, [k1/2e] 3 times, rm, inc1, pm, [k1/2e] 3 times, k1, p1—14 sts

Row 8: Inc1, k2, [k1/2e] 4 times, k1, rm, inc1, pm, k1, [k1/2e] 4 times, k2, p1—18 sts

Row 10: K4, [k1/2e] 4 times, k1, rm, inc1, pm, k1, [k1/2e] 4 times, k3, p2tog. Note: From this point on you will maintain 20 sts, not counting the "e" sts.

Rows 11, 13, 15: K to marker, purling all e sts, rm, inc1, k to last 2 sts, purling all e sts, p2tog.

Row 12: K3, [k1/2e] 4 times, k1, k1/2e, rm, inc1, pm, k1/2e, k1, [k1/2e] 4 times, k2, p2tog.

Row 14: K2, [k1/2e] 4 times, k1, k1/2e, k1 rm, inc1, pm, k1, k1/2e, k1, [k1/2e] 4 times, k1, p2tog.

Row 16: K1, [k1/2e] 4 times, k1, k1/2e, k1, k1/2e, rm, inc1, pm, k1/2e, k1, k1/2e, k1, [k1/2e] 4 times, purl remaining sts tog

Rows 17, 19: K to marker, purling all e sts, rm, inc1, pm, k to last 4 sts (2e + 2 sts), purl remaining sts tog.

Row 18: K1, [k1/2e] 3 times, k1, k1/2e, k1, k1/2e, k1, rm, inc1, pm, k1, k1/2e, k1, k1/2e, k1, [k1/2e] 3 times, purl remaining sts tog (2e + 2 sts).

Note: After Row 19, both sides will now be worked and bound off separately as follows:

ENDING SIDE 1

Row 1: K1, [k1/2e] 2 times, k1, k1/2e, k1, k1/2e, k3, turn—10 sts.

Row 2: Skp, k6, purling all e sts, purl tog 2e + last 2sts.

Row 3: K1, k1/2e, k1, k1/2e, k1, k1/2e, k2, turn—8 sts.

Row 4: Skp, k4, purling all e sts, purl tog 2e + last 2sts.

Row 5: K2, k1/2e, k1, k1/2e, k1, turn—6 sts.

Row 6: Skp (work this over 1 st + 2e + 1 sts), k2 purling 2 e sts, p2tog—4 sts.

Row 7: K1, k1/2e, k2, turn.

Row 8: Skp, purl tog 2e + last 2sts.

Row 9: K2.

Row 10: Skp, cut yarn and pull through last st.

ENDING SIDE 2

Attach yarn to topmost stitch at midpoint of work.

Row 1: K3, k1/2e, k1, k1/2e, k1, [k1/2e] 2 times, purl tog 2e + last 2sts—10 sts.

Row 2: K8, purling all e sts, p2tog—9 sts.

Row 3: K2, k1/2e, [k1, k1/2e] 2 times, purl tog 1 st + 2e + 1 st—8 sts.

Row 4: K6, purling all e sts, p2tog—7 sts.

Row 5: K1, k1/2e, k1, k1/2e, k1, p2tog—6 sts

Row 6: K4, purl tog 2e + last 2sts.

Row 7: K2, k1/2e, p2tog—4 sts.

Row 8: K2, purling all e sts, p2tog.

Row 9: K21, purl tog 1 st + 2e + 1 st. p2+2e tog (purling together 2 +2e sts making 1 stitch)—2 sts.

Row 10: Skp. Cut yarn and pull through last st. Weave in ends.

Mixed Cables

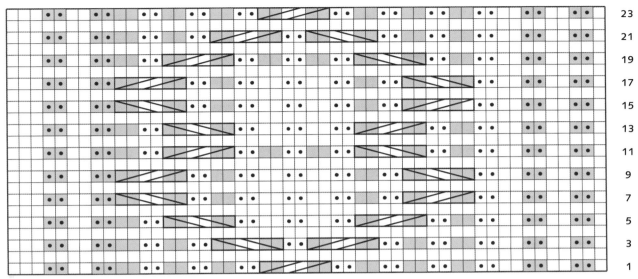

Front

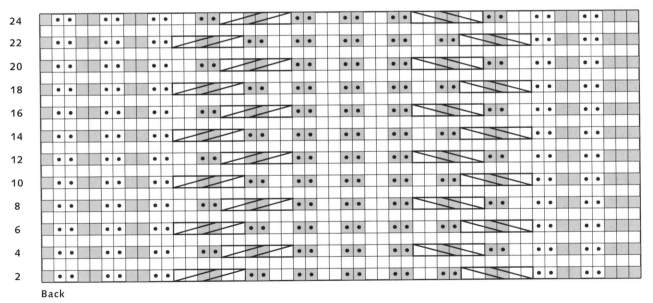

Back

	Knit with A		C2/1/2F k2B, p2A, k2B		C2/1/2F k2A, p2B, k2A
•	Purl with A				
	Knit with B		C2/1/2B k2B, p2A, k2B		C2/1/2B k2A, p2B, k2A
•	Purl with B				

YARN SUBSTITUTION CHART

Near the beginning of each project in this book, you'll find the weight, material, and color of each yarn in the piece shown. At the end of the project, you'll find the name and number of the specific yarns from Artyarns, Inc. (www.artyarns.com) that were used. The following chart provides a number of yarn varieties from other manufacturers that are the equivalent weight and composition of those from Artyarns.

Yarn in Project	Weight	Substitute Yarns
Artyarns Beaded Cashmere	**3** LIGHT	Lazer FX by Berroco held with Artyarns Cashmere 2 (or substitute) Beaded Merino/Silk by Angora Cottage Paillette by KFI held with Artyarns Cashmere 2 (or substitute)
Artyarns Beaded Silk	**3** LIGHT	Sequins by Great Adirondack Rock Star by Tilli Thomas Lazer FX by Berroco held with Artyarns Regal Silk (or substitute) Paillette by KFI held with Artyarns Regal Silk (or substitute) Reflections Sequins Novelty Yarn by Judi & Co.
Artyarns Cameo (or substitute)	**3** LIGHT	Hold Artyarns Cashmere 2 (or substitute) with a strand of Artyarns Silk Mohair
Artyarns Cashmere 1	**1** SUPER FINE	Superior by Filatura di Crosa Any Cashmere A by Habu Suri Elegance by America's Alpaca Grace by Blue Moon Fiber Arts Cashmere Colors Laceweight by Cherry Tree Hill Peruvian Baby Lace Merino by Elann Cobwebs by Great Adirondack Alpaca Lace by Misty Mountain Alpaca Silk by Valley Yarns
Artyarns Cashmere 2	**2** FINE	Monarch by Alchemy Cashmere by Bernat Peruvian Baby Cashmere by Elann Mongolian Cashmere by Jade Sapphire Light-Weight Cashmere by Karabella Supercashmere Fine by Karabella Seta/Cashmere by Lana Grossa Classic Cashcotton 4 Ply by Rowan Classic Cashsoft 4 Ply by Rowan Cachemir Anny by Anny Blatt
Artyarns Cashmere 5	**4** MEDIUM	Inspiration by Classic Elite Mongolian Cashmere by Jade Sapphire Pure Cashmere by K1C2 Lavish by Classic Elite Whale of a Skein by Lobster Pot Yarns Cashmel by Noro Cashmerino by Debbie Bliss Cashmere by Prism Cashmere Handspun by Trendsetter
Artyarns Ensemble (or substitute)	**4** MEDIUM	Hold any Artyarns Cashmere 1 (or substitute) with a strand of Artyarns Regal Silk
Artyarns Regal Silk and Artyarns Silk Pearl	**2** FINE	Pure Silk by Debbie Bliss Silk Purse by Alchemy Luxury by Filatura di Crosa Shangri La by Bouton d'Or Silky Wool by Elsebeth Lavold Tao by Colinette La Luz by Fiesta Pure & Simple by Tilli Thomas Tussah Silk by Tess Amerah by South West Trading Company

Yarn in Project	Weight	Substitute Yarns
Artyarns Silk Ribbon	**2** FINE	Any Artyarns Regal Silk (or substitute)
Artyarns Silk Mohair	**1** SUPER FINE	Kid Mohair by Adriafil Kidsilk Haze by Rowan Extra Fine Mohair by Be Sweet Kid Seta by Madil Douceur et Soie by K1C2 Any Silk Mohair A by Habu Mohair Luxe by Lang Parisienne by Colinette Super Kydd by Elann Baby Kid Extra by Filatura Di Crosa
Artyarns Supermerino	**4** MEDIUM	220 Wool by Cascade Classic Merino Wool by Patons Kureyon by Noro Sugar'n Cream by Lily Lamb's Pride Worsted by Brown Sheep Merino Worsted by Malabrigo Simply Soft by Caron Silk Garden by Noro Shepherd Worsted by Lorna's Laces Merino by Lana Grossa
Artyarns Ultramerino 4	**2** FINE	Koigu Painter's Palette Premium Merino (KPPPM) by Koigu Shepherd Sock by Lorna's Laces Zarina by Filatura di Crosa Sassy Stripes by Cascade Socks that Rock by Blue Moon Fiber Arts Basic Merino Socks by Fleece Artist Supersock by Cherry Tree Hill Soxie by Great Adirondack Saki by Prism Any Trekking by Zitron
Artyarns Ultramerino 6	**3** LIGHT	Zara by Filatura di Crosa Sport Weight by Blue Sky Princess Anny by Anny Blatt Mernos Sei by Baruffa Rialto by Debbie Bliss Merinogold by Grignasco Kersti by Koigu Margrite by Karabella Cashmere Plus by Lana Grossa Extrafine 4 Ply Merino by Mondial
Artyarns Ultramerino 8	**4** MEDIUM	220 Wool by Cascade Classic Merino Wool by Patons Kureyon by Noro Simply Soft by Caron Silk Garden by Noro Sugar'n Cream by Lily Lamb's Pride Worsted by Brown Sheep Merino Worsted by Malabrigo Aurora 8 by Karabella Handspun Wool by Manos Del Uruguay

ACKNOWLEDGMENTS

In the knitting world, certain yarn mavens have developed various tricks and techniques to create knitting that looks lovely on both sides. I have been inspired by Lily Chin's reversible cables, Jane Neighbors' slip stitch knitting, and Mary Lee Herrick, who compiled an online listing of reversible stitch patterns for Barbara Walker's *Treasury of Knitting Patterns* series. In addition, I've discovered some new talent online. For example, there is some very complex double knitting happening at www.fallingblox.com that is truly a feast for the eyes. Thanks also to Cat Bordhi, for making me aware of the möbius concept. Lisa Hoffman showed me a simple circular knitted scarf design that inspired several projects here. Shirley Paden, I will forever be grateful for all you have taught me.

Patty Dee, Dorothy Friedman, Linda Higham, and Judi Tepper—thanks for helping me to knit the projects and swatches. I couldn't have done it without you. Fanny, once again you helped me with the test knitting and I am most grateful. And Ruth, thank you for helping with last-minute projects.

Suzanne Tourtillott, my editor, took me by the hand and helped me through my most difficult moments, inspiring me to create some of the projects in the book and reorganize my approach. Thanks for your brilliant input. Judith Durant, my technical editor, did an amazing job of standardizing my project instructions and recreating my charts so that they would be clean and easy to follow. Thanks to editors Larry Shea, Nathalie Mornu, and Mark Bloom for juggling through my photos, illustrations, and taking care of those difficult details. Dana Irwin, as in our previous book collaborations, your visuals are spectacular. And over-the-top kudos to the entire Lark team for all their hard work.

I appreciate all the donations of needles and supplies from Jim and Terry at Colonial Needle. And the encouragement and support from so many wonderful shop owners and talented designers, including Cynthia, Laurie, Sharon, Lynda, Linda, Miriam, Hollis, Lynn, Edith, Beryl, Amy, and others.

Last but not least, I'd like to thank my husband and my two boys for tolerating my hectic schedule. They are so supportive and loving just when I need it most. I feel very lucky to have them in my life.

ABOUT THE AUTHOR

Iris Schreier is the author of *Lacy Little Knits* (Lark, 2007), *Modular Knits* (Lark, 2005) and co-author of *Exquisite Little Knits* (Lark, 2004). Her original, innovative techniques are used in knitting workshops around the world, and her patterns have been translated into multiple languages. In addition to appearing on Shay Pendray's *Needle Arts Studio* television program, she's been a repeat guest on *Knitty Gritty*. Iris has written articles and published patterns for leading knitting magazines as well. She is the founder of a popular Yahoo group focused on Multidirectional Knitting. The luxurious handpainted fibers featured in her unique patterns and designs were developed by Iris and are available through her company Artyarns. To view more of her designs, visit www.artyarns.com. Iris lives and works in White Plains, New York.

INDEX